The Vacation Rental Goldmine

How to Maximize Your Rental Income with Great Guest Experiences

© 2014 by Chris DeBusk

Cover Photo by Quoc Nguyen
Author Photo by Kathy Taylor Scott, www.kathytaylorscott.com
Illustrations by Sigit Pardiyanto

Table of Contents

I. Introduction

I started renting my vacation property a few years ago, taking properties with mediocre rental returns and making them exceptional rental producers – tripling or quadrupling the previous owner's gross rental income. Since you purchased <u>The Vacation Rental Goldmine,</u> I assume that you, too, are looking to maximize your rental return. My hope is that you can put this system to work for you with minimal effort. After watching a few friends succeed, I decided to share the system with everyone. They, too, had rental income results that exceeded what they thought possible.

What Makes This Book & System Different?

This book is written from the guest's perspective. It's a guide to creating great guest experiences as the pathway to maximizing income from your vacation rental. Each chapter starts with the guest and discusses what owners can and should do to make their experiences great. Other books on this topic are written almost solely from the owner perspective. They cover subjects like "Choosing Renters," or focus chapters on complaints or damages. Sure, these are important topics, but there is a big difference between doing things "to" renters and doing things "for" guests. A great guest experience results in improved guest retention, more bookings, and higher rates; all of which puts more money in your pocket!

Secondly, the Goldmine System provides detailed instructions and tools to bring great guest experiences to life. Other books on vacation rentals cover concepts, but leave the reader to figure out how to make it happen. The reader has to tackle the tough job of putting the concepts into practice, alone! As an example, many books cover the importance of a vacation rental website. The author typically concludes the topic by pointing out a couple of website building tools that are as easy to use as Microsoft Word®. I suspect most readers take a quick look at these tools and conclude they don't know how to get started. The Goldmine Toolkit contains detailed, step-by-step instructions on how to design, build and maintain a great vacation rental website. You don't have to be technical to do this, but it isn't as easy as Microsoft Word®. Creating a great guest experience takes work, but each concept is explained systematically to give you the tools to make it happen.

Lastly, I am here to help you, not just while you are reading the book, but also as you are putting your system into action. If you have questions about any aspect of the Goldmine System, please send an email to chris@vacationrentalgoldmine.com. I am happy to help in any way I can. I am extremely interested in your success, so whether it's a question, feedback or anything else, I look forward to hearing from you.

How Great Guest Experience Makes You the Most Money

Profit in business comes from repeat customers; customers that boast about your product and service, and that bring friends with them. – W. Edwards Deming

The vacation rental marketplace has exploded in recent years. This means lots of competition for all owners. VRBO and HomeAway have over 259,000 listings in the United States alone.

Fortunately, these aren't all in our vacation areas! Even with massive shifts to the rent by owner marketplace, rental companies still maintain a strong presence. Guests have more options than ever, and as owners, our competition has never been greater. To maximize rental income, a property really has to stand out from the pack.

Good news! The vacation rental industry isn't known for great guest experience, and with the right planning and local support, standing out is not terribly difficult. However, it does require an investment of time and money. For all the change in the vacation rental industry, much of the guest experience is designed with the interest of owners and rental companies at the forefront. Guests have learned through the years to tolerate the inconveniences, extra work, or perhaps even difficulty getting in touch with someone to help. Clear demonstration of interest in the guest, flexibility, and convenience go a long way toward standing out from the crowd.

So how does this translate into more dollars? When you successfully stand out from the crowd, your percentage of bookings from returning guests goes way up. This fills your calendar nicely and well in advance. Returning guests know you stand out from the crowd and are very likely to stay with you as you gradually raise your rates. After all, it's worth every penny for this vacation experience! For the remaining time on the calendar, new guests will shop your listing and see how booked the place is, as well as read your great reviews. Delighted guests are very willing to give you stellar reviews on the listing site. This is especially the case if you spend time cultivating these reviews. So, the new guests shopping your listing will see a full calendar and read exceptional reviews, which will get them booking. The net effect is booking more weeks at a higher rate: more profit! Voila, success begets success!

It may not happen overnight, but through multiple rental seasons, you can raise your rates and continue booking the most weeks for the most dollars. Everyone wins in this model, as your guests are thrilled, and you, the owner, are getting the greatest return possible. The rest of the book will focus on how to make this happen.

When we discuss the guest experience in the pages that follow, we will do so starting from the moment your guest begins looking for your listing. From that point forward, the hope is that your guest's experience just repeats over and over as they return to your home for many stays. They become a loyal guest whose emotional connection to your property grows through the years.

The Voice of the Guest

Throughout this book, you will see quotes labeled with "The Voice of the Guest." These are verbatim quotes from guests who have experienced the Goldmine System. The absolute best way to know if your guest experience is hitting the mark is to ask and listen. What better way to frame these experiences than in the exact words of the guests for which they are created? Ultimately, higher rental rates should go to better vacation rental "products." There are many great vacation rental options out there and you need yours to really stand out from the pack to get more dollars. Since your property is one of those great options, providing great guest service is the path to differentiate your property. Put these steps into play and watch your guests rave about their experiences, not just that you have a great place, but that you and the service they received are the best of any vacation rental.

Why a Vacation Rental Goldmine?

All owners would love to "strike it rich" with their vacation home, but there is more to the goldmine concept. In mining, Gold can be found anywhere from the soil surface to hundreds of feet down, below layers of rock. The surface provides smaller yields, while the bigger treasures are deep below, where few can reach. Surface mining tools include crude chisels and pans, while going deep requires specialized tools. Getting the most from your Vacation Rental Goldmine requires great tools and persistence to get below the surface to uncover the greatest riches. The Goldmine Toolkit gives you the tools to go after this big treasure.

How to Use the Book & Goldmine Toolkit

The Goldmine System consists of this book and optional Goldmine Toolkit. I sell them separately, so readers can get this book and its ideas at a low cost. Most concepts can be put into action just by reading the book. Without the toolkit, you have to put in the hours to create your own tools. Reading the book before purchasing the toolkit allows you to decide if you like the system before making an additional investment. My hope is that every owner will appreciate the option, but ultimately love the power of the system and purchase the toolkit as well. With it, you not only save countless hours, but more importantly, you will be more effective implementing the system.

Chapters in this book are ordered by the guest experience, from shopping online all the way through to post vacation. My hope is that you will read each chapter in order; however, you can dig into any chapter in the order you choose. Chapters 1 & 2 are important foundations, focusing on the guest experience and your marketing plan. As both are often referenced in other chapters, I strongly recommend reading those first and then focusing on specific areas from there, as desired.

The Goldmine Toolkit is available for purchase and download at www.vacationrentalgoldmine.com. It includes all the materials needed to create a great guest experience. This includes all Marketing, Communications, Financial Tracking, Dashboards and step-by-step documents. The Goldmine Toolkit can be purchased on the site and login credentials will be sent to provide access. The files in the kit are referenced by name throughout the book, and it's best to have them while you read each chapter. As for the financial spreadsheets and communications templates, you can start using them right away. You purchased a whole system you can use to maximize your rental income and create an awesome experience for your rental guests. This isn't about reading ideas and trying to figure out how to implement them on your own. The details you need to get going are included, so let's get started!

Chapter 1 – Create a Vacation Rental Marketing Plan

"Doing business without advertising is like winking at a girl in the dark. You know what you are doing, but nobody else does."

— Steuart Henderson Britt

So why bother with the formality of creating a Marketing Plan? It sounds like a lot of work, doesn't it? It's just answering some basic questions, which don't need big presentations or fancy formatting. Simply put, the Marketing Plan answers the questions of who you will market to and how you will do it. It's too important to leave to chance things like who you would like to have as guests, how much you will charge them, and how much you will spend on marketing. Vacation rental marketing can get expensive fast, so it's essential to invest your dollars for maximum results.

The Goldmine Toolkit includes a Vacation Rental Marketing Plan Template to guide you through key questions that should take about an hour. The plan template lists each question and has a spot for your answers, including a column titled Marketing Action. Based on your answer, the Marketing Action is what you plan to do, marketing wise with your answer. Actions could range from nothing, to making it a key element of your plan by prominent inclusion in your listing, etc.

What Are Your Vacation Rental Financial Goals?

It's important to know your financial goals when renting your vacation home. For the rest of this book, I assume you are trying to maximize your rental income; however, there isn't a right answer. Some owners just want to rent occasionally to help with basic expenses; it's unlikely they would purchase this book. Your goals shape every aspect of marketing and operating your vacation rental. If you want to pick up the occasional rental with limited wear and tear on your property, you will price, operate and market your rental very differently than if maximizing income is the goal.

Covering the mortgage can be a good initial goal. Using the Marketing Plan Worksheet, capture a couple sentences on your goal. Consider your Marketing Actions with the goal in the forefront of your mind. If you are renting only to cover expenses, you might just list at the basic tier on VRBO. For maximum rental income, you may instead decide to purchase the top tier on VRBO. Take a hard look at your financial goals, and make sure your marketing investment matches.

How Developed is Your Rental Market?

Assess the supply of vacation rentals in your area. Are there lots of vacation rentals out there, or just a few? The simplest way to find out is to go to VRBO/HomeAway and see how many listings there are. If the answer is in the thousands, you are in a developed rental market. If this is the case, standing out will be more challenging. If your area has a less developed rental market, with listings in the hundreds, this may play to your favor as minor adjustments in marketing expenditure could create big property visibility.

It's also good to know how many traditional rental companies are in your area. If rental companies are big players in the market, using a rental company with your rent by owner marketing may be a winning combination. Is the vacation rental supply in the area increasing or decreasing? This may be tough to know, but ask the locals who work in real estate or with rental companies. You may decide lots of rental properties in the local market means listing on multiple sites at higher tiers. In a less crowded rental marketplace, higher listing tiers could result in extremely good search placement.

What's Great about Your Vacation Rental Property?

No one knows your property better than you do, and you know why you bought it. On the Marketing Plan Worksheet, make a list of 6-8 great things about your property. Once you get going, I bet this list begins to build quickly. Here are a few starter questions:

1. Do you have a great view?
2. Are you near desirable attractions?
3. Are there big advantages to your setting?
4. Do you have great outdoor features to your home – such as decks/balconies/pool?
5. Does the interior have modern furnishings?
6. Does the Kitchen have modern appliances, countertops, cabinets?
7. Is the size of your home good for certain guest parties – two families, great for kids?
8. How is the technology in the property – specifically the TVs and entertainment options?
9. Nice mattresses?

When we bought our first property, here is the list I came up with:

1. Fantastic long-range view of water and golf course
2. Located in the center of a desirable vacation destination
3. Serene/peaceful setting
4. Large deck and balcony
5. Great size for two families
6. Great for kids – trundle beds
7. A bike ride to the beach

We will revisit this list later in the book when we discuss effective listings and web content. Make the strengths of your vacation property evident in the pictures, marketing text and guest communications. After you feel you have a good list, order it by degree of importance. Given the importance of these characteristics, it's likely you will have a Marketing Action that highlights these characteristics in pictures or listing text.

What Sets Your Property Apart From the Competition?

Looking back through your list of strengths above, determine which of these is unique to your property. Your list has things you love about your property, but are they unique? If you don't come up with much that is unique, then think through which of the strengths are rare. If your place has a great deck that stands out, but one other owner in your neighborhood has it too, then go ahead and advertise it as a key feature. For Marketing Action, you will likely want to showcase a unique feature in most or all of your marketing. For example, if you have a completely awesome view, this should be your main listing picture to catch the eyes of your prospective guests.

What Could Be Better About Your Property?

This may seem a strange question for a marketing plan, but it is important to think through whether any of your property opportunities should be considered in your marketing. Depending on the significance of the issues, lower your price or make certain prospective guests know what they are getting when they rent your home. Through time, you may decide to invest in improvements for some of these items.

When we purchased our first vacation home, here is the opportunities list I came up with:
1. Dated interior and decorations
2. Old appliances
3. TVs and technology from another decade
4. Poor interior maintenance
5. Old flooring

Decide whether these items need to be addressed, and if so, when you plan to do it. No vacation home is perfect and if these things don't measure up to your standards, chances are others *may* feel the same. As an owner, you should be ready to hear feedback on your property opportunities, and the good news is, now you have a plan.

As I am sure you will agree, honesty with guests is of the utmost importance, so always be factually accurate. That said, things that bother you might not be a big deal to your guests. Remember that you probably spend a lot of time there and may be the type of person who notices everything. Be honest in your opportunity assessment and be open to guest feedback as to what matters to them.

Old appliances was on the opportunities list above, and based on cost we didn't replace until after we owned our first property for a bit over a year. I didn't add "old appliances" in our listing text, but I didn't hide anything, either. I made sure the kitchen pictures showed the appliances, so no guest would ever be surprised. All the appliances worked fine, but by most standards, they were old. If the older appliances were a big deal, they could move onto another property with newer appliances. No guest ever gave feedback that the appliances were old, but if they had, I would have been ready. I would have graciously thanked them for their feedback and then quickly mentioned that we planned to update the appliances to stainless in the winter of that year. In addition, I would mention that I hoped they would return to see and use those new appliances.

Some opportunities on your list may be ones that can't be changed. For example, say your home was further from the beach than you would like. This is a case where an opportunity could actually be a strength to some guests. While lots of folks like to stay on the beach, some like to be near it but off the beaten path. If your place is like this, you could do the following:

1. State the actual distance to the beach
2. Point out that it is a bike ride
3. Focus on the peaceful and secluded vacation surroundings

Give your prospective guests the facts to make an informed decision. The last thing anyone wants is a vacation ruined by misunderstanding or misinformation. Poor guest experiences and reviews can be tough to bounce back from. Give your guests an accurate representation of your property so they can decide and encourage their questions upfront. With this in mind, go through your list of opportunities to see if you feel any of them warrant a Marketing Action.

What Types of Guests Do You Want to Attract?

Paying guests are usually great, but knowing to whom your vacation home has most appeal can help you focus on those key features. Done effectively, this should result in these target guests really wanting to rent it. Are you looking to attract families, retired folks, or couples looking for a getaway? The answer to this question should influence what you offer in your property and how you talk about it in your listing and communications. It's not that you wouldn't appreciate other guests, but if you could pick your ideal demographics what would they be?

With my properties, I have two target demographics. Families are a big focus based on the size of my properties, and I have trundle beds in the kid's rooms to appeal to them. I can house two families looking to vacation together by accommodating up to four kids. Also, stocking some kid's games and books is a good way to really make them feel welcome while vacationing. My second demographic is vacationing, retired couples. Not only do these couples have the time to travel throughout the year, but they also tend to take exceptionally good care of your home. Less wear and tear is less expense. To appeal to them, I highlight the serenity of the setting and convenience of leisure activities.

How Are You Pricing Your Property and Why?

Proper rental pricing maximizes value for your guests and revenue for you. A thoughtful and flexible approach to pricing can make all the difference between a full rental schedule of happy guests and your place sitting empty instead of earning for you.

Before we dig into analyzing pricing in your area, focus on the guest to understand their motivations. Why do prospective guests go the vacation rental by owner route?

1. To get a good deal
2. There are lots of choices
3. Vacation rental by owner sites are easy to find
4. Believe vacation experience will be better dealing directly with owner

This list is likely not exhaustive, but I bet one or more of the above apply to a great majority of rent-by-owner guests. The first three factors on the above list underscore how important pricing is in the eyes of prospective guests. This is a very price-sensitive crowd. If guests are looking for a good deal where they have lots of options, the challenge is to stand out with a great offering at a good price.

Knowing this, how does it inform my pricing strategy? It certainly doesn't mean you need to "give it away," but instead implies that homework and experimentation with pricing is critical. So with that, let's get started analyzing the marketplace a bit to get the pricing right.

Great news! There is lots of great competitive data for you just a few clicks away. Use VRBO, HomeAway, or whatever listing site you believe will be your primary marketplace, along with the Goldmine Pricing Analyzer. VRBO tends to be best as it has the most listings and powerful filtering tools to make your job getting competitive data easier. In most cases, you will be able to see your competition's calendar to see how they are doing with their bookings at different price points.

The Pricing Analyzer helps you capture comparison-pricing data for like properties in your area, similarly to how property appraisers gather comparables as part of the home purchase process. Next, gather pricing and booking performance data on five or more like properties in your area to assess how your pricing stacks up, or to determine a solid starting point.

Once you are on your listing site, filter down to your vacation area in its state so you get a broad return of listings, as opposed to just inside your resort or city. VRBO has really advanced filtering tools that allow you to add location type, property type, and number of bathrooms to really narrow your search to similar properties. Bedrooms, bathrooms, and setting are amongst the most important factors to make sure are the same in comparable vacation properties. After including a few in the general area, find some neighboring properties or similar ones in your resort area.

Once you get a good list, begin looking through some of the properties to narrow down on ones that really look similar to yours, have good rate information available, and view their calendars so you can see bookings. Enter the listing numbers of these properties in the Analyzer and bookmark them as you go so you can come back easily for data gathering. Right now, you are just creating a solid list. Loosen the filters slightly if you need additional properties to get to a list of about six. You can also head to a local rental company site to get some comparison properties there as well.

Now that you have your comparable property list, start gathering more detailed data. The analyzer allows you to capture pricing by season, rating similarity to your property, and rating booking performance. You will be making judgments during data entry, so try to use the same criteria when rating each property.

To keep things simple, you will gather average pricing for each of the four seasons, including nightly and weekly pricing if applicable. For the Property Similarity ranking, use the following scale:
1. Extremely Similar
2. Somewhat Similar

For Booking Performance, use the following scale looking at a four to six month timeframe:
1. Excellent Bookings – A full or relatively full calendar
2. Average Bookings – Bookings spaced out through time
3. Poor Bookings – Significant gaps or low bookings

For Guest Experience, use the following scale:
1. Excellent Reviews
2. Average Reviews
3. Poor Reviews – Anything less than all positive reviews should not be included

Depending on the time of year, seasonality may play a factor. Consider those as best you can. The other good news is that you should refresh this view by tracking these properties a few times throughout the year to see any pricing or booking performance changes.

Now that you have your data, there are a few useful ways to employ it:

1. Closely analyze any properties that got a 1 rating for both similarity and excellent bookings. You may want to mirror their pricing, or go with something close.
2. Study the pricing of all Property Similarity Rating 1 to get an idea of the range and where yours falls.
3. Analyze any Booking Performance Rating 3 properties to see if you can identify why they may be underperforming. Assess where their pricing is and whether that may be the issue. Analyzing the poor performers will hopefully help avoid pitfalls.

Now, you should have sufficient data to evaluate your pricing relative to the competition. If you are just starting out, it may be wise to price right at the average or slightly below. With more time in market and great guest experience, you can begin to move your pricing a bit above the average.

Give particular focus on properties that you gave 1 ratings to in both similarity and performance. If for some reason, you don't have valuable insight based on the six or so properties, add some. You could also swap out some that you find not to be worthwhile comparisons. Having analyzed properties in the area, you can set your own pricing with the knowledge you based it on market research. On the Marketing Plan Worksheet, note your pricing strategy and your Marketing Action to revise or update your pricing.

Not very many comps in the area 11/18.

Where Will You Spend Your Precious Marketing Dollars?

Before answering this question, think through how prospective guests shop for vacation rentals at your destination. While many guests know about VRBO or HomeAway, search engines play a big role in driving prospective guest traffic. Many guests use Google as their starting point, <u>and you clearly want your listing to be where the crowds are.</u>

To help with data capture for some quick analysis on how search engines treat your vacation destination, the Goldmine Toolkit includes a Search Engine Marketing Worksheet. We are going to focus on the top three search results for a number of keywords that folks use, as these are the big players in your vacation area. We will search various keywords on the top three search engines as ranked by comScore – Google, Bing, and Yahoo.[1] Google's dominance of search is difficult to overstate at 65% of all searches, so it's clearly is the most important to watch.

Start with a simple example using Cape Cod as our destination. Guests looking for a vacation rental at Cape Cod likely search with something like:

> Cape Cod Vacation Rental
> Cape Cod Rental
> Cape Cod Vacation Home Rental
> Cape Cod Vacation Homes for Rent

Using the first keywords in the list above, let's head to Google to

---

[1] comScore, "comScore Releases April 2014 Search Engine Rankings ," < https://www.comscore.com/Insights/Market_Rankings/comScore_Releases _April_2014_US_Search_Engine_Rankings> (accessed June 21, 2014).

do some searching. It is important to note that results are dynamic over time; however, the top s vacation destinations show some consistency.

"Cape Cod Vacation Rental" brings up HomeAway, VRBO, and TripAdvisor as the top three at the time of writing. The same search on Bing yields capecodrentals.com, HomeAway, and VRBO. Heading back to Google, the search for "Cape Cod Rental" results with HomeAway, VRBO and weneedavacation.com.

Now, substitute your vacation destination using the keywords above, and feel free to add some additional ones. Write down the search results in order for each keyword combination, while noting the order of the top three results returned. While you may find a local site or two that pop up in the top three, I imagine you found HomeAway.com and VRBO.com most frequently. Take a couple keyword combinations to Bing to see if you get similar results.

In just a few minutes, you've gained valuable insight into how search engines drive traffic to listing sites for your vacation destination. Throughout this book, you will feel me urge you to invest as much as you can, and more, in getting a great listing search position where your prospective guests are. If VRBO and HomeAway are the top sites on Google, one or both of them deserve consideration for significant listing spending. We will cover this in great detail in the next chapter. For now, take a moment to jot down where you plan to advertise your vacation rental and at what level of subscription, on the Marketing Plan Worksheet. An investment of 5% or more of your gross rentals is a good rule of thumb.

.ow, the first cut of your marketing plan is complete. This was important foundational work, as you clearly articulated what differentiates your property, your target guests, your pricing strategy, and how you plan to promote your property. The Guest Experience starts with good Marketing. Guests need to be able to find your property and understand its great features to begin experiencing it. Their experience begins with the first view of your listing and hopefully ends with happy vacationers raving about how excellent it was and planning their return.

Gold Mining Tips

1. **Create a simple Marketing Plan using the Vacation Rental Marketing Plan Template to decide who you will market to and how.**
2. **Determine your financial goals, as they impact your marketing investment and pricing.**
3. **Make a list of great things about your vacation property to promote.**
4. **Understand what is unique about your property versus the competition.**
5. **Identify your guest target audience to determine which features to promote.**
6. **Use the Pricing Analyzer to purposefully set your rental pricing.**
7. **Choose listing sites by studying search engine results for your vacation area.**
8. **Invest as heavily as you can afford with listings where the masses are.**

Chapter 2 – Guest Experience Really Matters!

"We are Ladies & Gentlemen serving Ladies and Gentlemen"

- Ritz Carlton Motto

Great guest service can really make your property stand out. The vacation rental industry frankly isn't known for delivering it, and guests have grown accustomed to generally low levels of service. Most books on vacation rental success are written from the owner's perspective and include chapters like "Picking your guests." This is not to suggest that guest screening should be abandoned, but you shouldn't think of guests as an inconvenience. Without them, there is no vacation rental business. Make your guests feel valued and important, and watch them come back to your home again and again. This is so essential to maximizing your rental income that the remainder of the book is written from the guest perspective. We will cover topics in the order the guest experiences them, and discuss what owners can do to make them great.

The Changing Hospitality Industry

All owners are a very small part of a huge hospitality industry that has been redefining itself over the past few years. It has been particularly interesting to watch what hoteliers have been up to recently. Hotels clearly have gotten the message that the key to a thriving business is guest satisfaction. They have been investing significantly in service, and guest satisfaction is on the rise. Like them, our vacation rental industry would be wise to wake up to the same notion. We are in a super competitive business and

21

many owners' income is way under what it could be by settling for a "rental company cookie cutter" guest experience. Your bottom line can benefit in a big way from being purposeful about creating a great guest experience. Whether it's guests coming back, or marketing a great experience to prospective guests, it pays!

The Ritz Carlton Experience

According to the JD Power ratings, the Ritz Carlton is the gold standard in the hospitality industry.[2] If you have ever stayed at a Ritz, it's difficult to describe the experience as anything other than exceptional. The hotel facilities are top notch, but there is much more at work than that. The hotelier shares their credo, "The Ritz-Carlton experience enlivens the senses, instills well-being, and fulfills even the unexpressed wishes and needs of our guests."[3] This is indeed a high bar for the experience. The idea that the experience is so well designed and executed that it can fulfill even unexpressed wishes of guests seems game changing. The Ritz anticipates guest needs and creates the experience around it. This is an important concept that we will return to later.

---

[2] J.D. Power, "Following Two Years of Declines, Hotel Guest Satisfaction Increases to a Seven-Year High ," <http://www.jdpower.com/press-releases/2013-north-america-hotel-guest-satisfaction-index-study> (accessed June 18, 2014).

[3] "Ritz Carlton: About Us – Gold Standard," 2014 <http://corporate.ritzcarlton.com/en/About/GoldStandards.htm> (accessed June 18, 2014).

Taking a deeper look at the Ritz-Carlton service values for their employees gives additional insight into how they strive for excellence.[4]

1. I build strong relationships and create Ritz-Carlton guests for life.
2. I am always responsive to the expressed and unexpressed wishes and needs of our guests.
3. I am empowered to create unique, memorable and personal experiences for our guests.
4. I continuously seek opportunities to innovate and improve The Ritz-Carlton experience.
5. I own and immediately resolve guest problems.
6. I create a work environment of teamwork and lateral service so that the needs of our guests and each other are met.
7. I am responsible for uncompromising levels of cleanliness and creating a safe and accident-free environment.

There are more service values in Ritz's list than what is above, but I found these directly applicable to us as vacation rental owners. Building guest relationships means connecting with your guests. Anticipating needs is designing a great experience for them. I bet you create great personal experiences at your vacation home, so help guests do that as well and never stop making it better. So much of the experience happens at the property; invest locally to make sure all the details are cared for.

---

[4] "Ritz Carlton: About Us – Gold Standard," 2014 <http://corporate.ritzcarlton.com/en/About/GoldStandards.htm> (accessed June 18, 2014).

What Experience Will You Create For Guests

"Every contact we have with a customer influences whether or not they'll come back. We have to be great every time or we'll lose them." – Kevin Stirtz

Considering the Ritz Carlton wisdom and using your own experience, spend a moment thinking through the experience you want to create for *your* guests. Keep it simple by writing statements about what you would like your guests to feel before, during, and after the vacation. It may help to think about a great vacation you had, and how you felt about it. Just spend a few minutes thinking through this. Here are a couple that should be on everyone's list to get started:

Guests feel the property is clean.
Guests feel the booking process is easy and convenient.

Please don't read the list below until you have created your own. Of course, use any of the experience feelings in my list that you wish, but remember that thinking through and wording your own will make them more personally relevant to you and your guests.

I came up with the following list, and I bet you have similar themes on your list as well.

Guests got what they expected and more from their vacation.
Guests feel that I, and everyone they interact with for the rental, care about their vacation.
Guests feel the booking process is easy and convenient.
Guests feel they know how to get the most out of their vacation time at the property.

Guests feel they always have someone to help if they need something.

Guests feel that the property is clean.

Guests feel that the property is modern and well maintained.

Guests feel the property is equipped with what they need, and more.

Guests feel they are getting a great value for the vacation dollar.

Guests feel that the overall experience is amongst the best they have had on vacation.

Now that you have a full list, compare it to what the hospitality industry experts say. JD Power, the voice of customers across countless industries, does an annual hospitality study of the hotel industry to determine which hoteliers have the best customer satisfaction.[5] They assess hotels on the following dimensions as the key factors of guest satisfaction:

Reservation

Check In/Check Out

Guest Room

Food & Beverage – Not generally applicable to vacation rentals

Hotel Services – Not generally applicable to vacation rentals

Hotel Facilities

Cost & Fees

From a quick comparison of the JD Power list with ours, it appears the bases are covered. Using the guest experience list you

---

[5] J.D. Power, "Following Two Years of Declines, Hotel Guest Satisfaction Increases to a Seven-Year High ," <http://www.jdpower.com/press-releases/2013-north-america-hotel-guest-satisfaction-index-study> (accessed June 18, 2014).

created, take a spin through your marketing plan to see if any updates are needed. Emphasizing aspects of your guest experience that are unique is a great way to stand out. Let prospective guests know in the listing you have no check in/out process to make it super easy, or you have cleaning inspections to make certain things are just so.

The Phases of Guest Experience

"Everything about this rental was wonderful, from initial booking to check out. Owner was extremely accessible prior to and during my trip. I have rented many times through VRBO in the past and this by far was the best experience we have had!" – Voice of the Guest

It can be quite an involved process for guests to shop for a property, book, and go on vacation. I have captured these steps in phases of the guest experience that will be used as an outline for much of the remainder of the book. Walking through the guest experience step-by-step will help you structure your desired experience for the greatest return. You will find recommendations and tools to use in each chapter that I hope will help up your game in marketing, communications, and operations of your vacation rental.

In simple terms, guests need to find a vacation spot, secure it at the right time, and go have a great time on vacation. Sometimes, it really is that simple. For many, however, it isn't. Most folks don't get to go on vacation very often, and it is a big deal. Many families take just one big vacation a year. This means guests do lots of research and diligence to make sure they get a great vacation that's affordable.

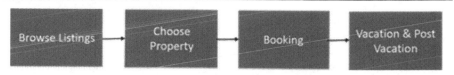

Browse Listings — Browsing is the first stage of vacation rental shopping. The guest is looking around the listing site to identify a set of suitable vacation home candidates. Depending on guest preferences and vacation area, this phase may be short or long. Either way, you want your listing to stand out if it is being considered.

The Browse Listing phase is like "window shopping" to see what is out there in their desired location and price bracket. Some guests skip window-shopping altogether and begin narrowing down options because they know what they are looking for.

Choose Property — The guest narrows the set of properties and may comparison-shop to make the best choice for their vacation party. Some shoppers will browse and choose at the same time, and others will want to extensively research before deciding what to book. Owners often play a role by answering questions via email or phone. These interactions can have significant impact on the decision to choose one property over another.

Booking — The guest has decided on the property and is ready to make the reservation. Booking includes deposit payment, rental agreement approval, and final payment.

Vacation & Post Vacation — The time for vacation has finally arrived, and the guest packs for the trip, travels to your home and begins vacationing. When the vacation unfortunately comes to an end, the guest travels home with the memories they created.

Many of you who have experience with vacation rentals know that no two guests go through these phases the same way. The recently implemented "Book It Now" feature on VRBO has made it easy for guests to do the first three phases in one web session. I truthfully can't say enough good things about how great that capability is for everyone. It is super easy for guests to book and be done, and how great for owners to receive a reservation and click "Accept." While the browse, select, and reserve phases are critically important, there is significant coverage in this book for the vacation phase itself. This is an area where I believe many owners don't invest enough.

Now, let's go through each phase with our guests!

Gold Mining Tips

1. **Make a list of experiences you will create for guests.**
2. **Promote these experiences in your listing as appropriate.**
3. **Follow the guest through the phases of the experience and take steps to make certain you are doing your best to create experiences on your list.**

Chapter 3 – Browse Listings – Draw Guests in With Experiences

"Buying is a profound pleasure."

- Simone de Beauvoire

Owners who have been in the rental market for a while are familiar with window shoppers. The internet has made browsing and shopping easier than ever! These guests are looking to see what they can afford in a particular vacation destination. Some vacation rental guests skip this step, as they know where they want to go and what they want. These folks move straight to narrowing their options. Guests are smart to test the market to get a deal.

The early stages of the search are a great time to stand out from your competition with a great property at a great price. While some guests shop from their browsers, many go ahead and send inquiries to understand their best prices early. Shot gunning is a practice where guests send lots of inquiries. It's easy to spot a shotgun inquiry as it is typically very short, not specific, and may include references that are not applicable to the property. Respond swiftly to likely shotgunners and get on with making a big impression on guests likely to rent your home.

Make Your Listing Stand Out

Start with fantastic photos. In addition to great photos, the top vacation rental listing sites have created excellent filtering tools. At this stage, price range is the most powerful of these. The

29

guest may have a very specific budget, and they are shopping to see what they can get at the destination within their budget.

When setting your pricing, make sure you have schooled yourself on your listing site's pricing filter ranges. The filters typically have the ranges preset. If you can find your way into a lower price range without sacrificing many dollars, that's a great strategy. You may also be able to edge your rate up without losing ground in the filter category. Long story short, make sure you price with the listing site filters in mind so that you get the most traffic early in the shopping process.

Help Your Guests Shop

At this stage of the search, prospective guests typically keep things simple by focusing on price and bedrooms based on the size of their party. When guests see a long list of prospective properties, how do they choose which ones to click on versus scroll by? This is where pictures and listing titles really matter. Your primary picture draws the guest in to your listing, or sends them scrolling. Back to the window shopping analogy – this is a visual exercise where the guests see what the "shopkeeper" has to offer. And sometimes, the window-shopped item becomes a real purchase.

So given the fact that the primary picture is so critical, how do you pick the best one? Break out the marketing plan you put together earlier in the book and look at the list of things that differentiate your property from the others in your area. Is your view dynamite? Is the front of your house quaint? Are you close to the beach? Interior modern and newly renovated? Center your picture on what sets your property apart and looks amazing.

With my properties, I showcase the views. Guests will typically be outside a lot while vacationing, and the view pictures give them a sense of the setting. Views from decks, patios, etc. are often a good choice. I don't generally recommend that the primary photo show an interior room unless it's exceptional. Vacationers spend limited time inside, and it's tough to make your property stand out with interior rooms. If you have something super modern and upscale, go for it. On average, most owners would be better served to focus elsewhere first. Vacationers will eventually investigate the interior pictures further before booking.

After picking a great photo, decide on a great listing title to match. The same principles apply: you should focus on unique features. If your title matches the photo, that's all the better. Usually, folks like great views, updated properties and proximity to fun things or attractions. If you call out something great in your title as a strength, it MUST be clearly showcased in your photos and easy to see. For example, if you say your property has a 'Breathtaking View with Many Updates', then the view in the pictures must be as fantastic. Many updates says new appliances/kitchen and modern decorating. If the pictures don't show this, credibility is lost and guests will quickly move on.

Draw the Window Shoppers In

It's easy to assume that window shoppers aren't serious vacation rental prospects, but this could result in big missed opportunities. While the prospective guest might just be "kicking tires," it's unlikely they thought spending their time looking on vacation rental sites would be worthwhile if they didn't plan on eventually taking a vacation. HomeAway has added Favorites to their website, which is a great tool for window shoppers. While quickly browsing listings, the guest can save property listings for later. The Favorites option is very prominent in the experience and displays the primary image upfront. Draw guests in with great pictures and experiential text that allows them to imagine themselves there.

Sometimes the window shopper will send you an inquiry that looks something like, "Please send me a quote with the total cost for this week." The best thing for a window shopper is to get quick access to information on your listing or a response to their inquiry. The pop you put into your photos or listing text is working to get the prospective guest interested. Whether it's this year or three years from now, a window shopper can be your next vacationing guest.

Gold Mining Tips

1. Invest in great photos to capture your guest's attention early.
2. Make sure the primary listing picture and title are both excellent.
3. Focus pictures and listing text on vacation experiences to draw in guests.

Chapter 4 – Choose Property – Know & Appeal to Prospective Guests

"The aim of marketing is to know and understand the customer so well the product or service fits and sells itself."

— *Peter Drucker*

At this stage, the guest has clearly decided to go on vacation and now needs to decide where they are staying. They have likely done research and have created a list of important requirements in their mind. Planning a vacation is fun, so share in that with your guests. It's impossible to predict each guest's requirements, but at the simplest level, most guests are looking for a nice home in a nice place at a good price. As your prospective guest chooses their vacation property, create a stronger connection to them by having some insight into who they are.

Who Are Your Prospective Guests?

As you begin to write or rewrite your listing, website, etc., think about what guests you are looking to attract and how they are likely to shop. During the first chapter, you spent time thinking through your ideal guests. These could be families, older couples, etc. Then, translate that into what type of shoppers you will have most browsing your listing.

It's likely that families and couples are in your target groups. At the risk of overgeneralization, women tend to be the planners and purchasers for households. On a percentage basis, greater than 50% of my inquiries and bookings come from women who are the ultimate purchasers in almost every household. This is an important factor to keep in mind as you craft your listing. If you have been at this a while, go back and look at your inquiry history to see your property trends. If you don't have a great percentage of women shoppers, it's important to know why. It may be that your locale and activities in the surrounding area have a big appeal to men. For example, my lake property gets quite a bit of traffic for weekend rentals in the off-season for fishing trips. Women do not tend to be into fishing. The biggest worry is that your listing is not appealing to the women who view it, so you are missing out on a big segment of vacation purchasers. This is tough to know for sure, because listing sites likely don't know or provide this level of detail in their web metrics. If you don't have many women inquiring and booking, you should look into refreshing things a bit. We will cover how below.

I have observed four main types of vacation shoppers. For those who have been doing vacation rental by owner for a while, I bet you will recognize many or all of these folks. By some educated guessing and your own experience, you can determine which of these you are seeing most or how to best appeal to segments you should be attracting. While a vacation purchaser may fit into multiple segments, these are intended to be the shopper's primary motivation through the process.

1. The Bargain Shopper – Everyone wants a good deal; however, these folks work harder at it than most. This segment is likely to shotgun out a lot of inquiries with a request for a "good rate." I suspect many shoppers are attracted to vacation rental by owner so they can get good pricing and potentially haggle. Rental companies may

haggle a bit, but generally, it's limited to protect their margins. If price is a big factor to guests, the rental company is much more likely to direct the guest to a different property in their inventory, because that's easier. I tend to not engage in a lot of discounting on request, so I don't convert a lot of these customers to rentals reactively. Discounting has a place, but I find it more effective when done proactively versus reactively. When guests ask for a discount, they are generally looking for something big, and if you are doing your rates right, you won't offer this. This strategy defies conventional wisdom about discounting in the industry. This wisdom would tell you, "Don't offer a discount until the guest asks for it." The biggest problem with this approach is most guests who don't like your price just move on. After all, they likely sent out lots of inquiries fishing for a great deal. Also, many guests might reserve with a discount, but won't ask and pick another property. If you want to discount, do a small discount proactively in the inquiry response to show the guest how welcome they are. This gesture can be very well received and just the thing that gets you the reservation versus your competition.

How to Appeal to Bargain Shoppers: As mentioned above, this segment is not one I recommend you spend much time trying to win. You are selling a differentiated experience with fair pricing, so stick to your guns on pricing unless you feel it's desirable, from your perspective, to discount. Filling a difficult off-season week, or getting a desirable demographic, is good examples of times to consider proactive discounts. Do

35

your homework on pricing, make your prices are fair/comparable, and decide when/if to provide proactive discounts.

2. The Researcher – Researchers study seemingly all aspects of vacation properties before making a decision. They are easy to recognize, as they ask many thoughtful questions about amenities and may tell you details of their trip and ask for your help. Thinking through how their grandkids can all be comfortable sleeping is an example. What kind of mattresses are on the beds? Do you have a stockpot and broiler in the kitchen? What type of laundry detergent does the washing machine require? It's time for another overgeneralization moment. As I mentioned above, women are the primary buyers of the family, so it's safe to say they will want to research before each big purchase as well. As common sense and many consumer behavior studies will tell you, "Men buy things; women shop." Men tend to have a narrow set of requirements and a short decision process, which may look like – "Nice view, enough bedrooms, this place will work." Researchers also tend to be older. They may have more time to investigate the finer points, and perhaps plan to stay longer at your property. If you are staying somewhere a month versus a week, it is logical to put more into investigating the place. A month would be a long time to regret a decision!

The most sophisticated researchers choose a property similarly to how businesses buy services through proposals or a request for proposal process. They do initial inquiries to a large set of owners who appear to meet their general requirements. Based on those responses, they narrow the properties down to a small number and really investigate those. If you are getting lots of questions from a particular guest, you are probably a finalist in their selection process!

One of my guests, Amanda, was shopping for a month-long stay, and compiled a list of seven potential properties to do her research. Amanda further researched and narrowed the list down to three before making her final decision. She emailed me numerous times through the process with new questions, which I promptly answered while encouraging more. Once she delivered the news that she was selecting our property, I asked her what factors were most important in her decision. Amanda said the website provided her so much more in terms of photos, floor plans, and information that she felt most confident with her decision.

How to Appeal to Researchers: Researchers crave information, especially in the final stages of their decision process. Good news though! They tend to be very willing to do the research on their own. Providing the details in your listing and on your website can pay big dividends. Make sure these details are easy to find, but optional for the non-Researchers out there. Give researchers big pictures of the areas of your vacation home and provide details on bed sizes, bed brands, towels, sheets, fireplace, outdoor amenities, etc. Don't add these items to the listing description, but spend time populating the listing details for researchers to opt into, so they can answer their own questions in the right sections. On the website, give researchers lots of data they can use, and bigger pictures to see things. As an example, a home floor plan can be a great add. Researchers may use this to think through where their kids and/or grandkids will sleep and hang out.

Always encourage researcher's questions! In every communication with all guests, ask them for their questions. Some researchers don't mind asking tons of questions, but others may feel like they are bothering owners. True encouragement of their questions makes them feel good about getting the information they need, and gives you an opportunity to connect with them. After all, most owners love talking about their property, and researchers love information! If you make yourself always available via email/phone, let guests know as they shop. Be extremely responsive and timely to their requests. If you have onsite support for them, this can be a big insurance policy against something bad happening during their vacation with no response. Researchers research so they don't have problems!

Keep in mind that researchers are doing comparison-shopping. Listen and respond to their needs. A vacation is a big deal to everyone, but it is a particularly big deal to these guests. Anything you can do to make them feel confident in their decision might just be the thing that helps them choose your place over the others.

3. The Convenience Shopper – Convenience shoppers want to get things done quickly. Also, they tend to like extra

38

services that make their vacations easier. It can be challenging to identify these guests, but they generally tend to be men. If you get an inquiry from a man with little to no content, they may be a convenience shopper. You may get questions about the check in/out process or how far away things are. These are solid clues you are talking to someone who values convenience. Convenience shoppers may also opt for an online-booking "Book It Now Option," which makes it easy for everyone. As an owner, what's better than reservations showing up with a rental agreement approved and deposit paid! Online reservations bring a smile to my face every time.

How to Appeal to Convenience Shoppers – Simply put, make things easy for guests and promote it in your listing. Simplify check in/out, reserving the property and getting help while on vacation. Eliminate the check in and check out process. It's awful to have to drive to an office somewhere to pick up some keys or passes, especially after you have been on the road for hours. Likewise, dropping things off the morning you are trying to get out of town is no fun, either. Make it easy for your guests to arrive and leave, as it saves a lot of work for everyone. Guests get to arrive and depart like they own the place! There is more on this topic in the vacation section.

The best listing sites have invested in tools to make managing reservations easy. Use them to streamline bookings and payments for both you and guests. Eliminate physical processing: no paper checks, paper rental agreements or security deposit checks. Digital tools make booking and payments convenient for guests and simple for owners.

While on vacation, give guests easy access to you and someone local to help them in the event they need something. Onsite property management comes at a cost, but pays dividends for you and your guests. It's difficult to manage a property and guest experience without eyes and ears on the ground. Local support goes a long way to make things worry free for your guests.

Advertise your no check in and out process and onsite property management in your listings and on the website. This will be appreciated by everyone, but will be of particular importance to these guests. When communicating to these guests, use language like, "to keep things easy, …." or "we try to make things simple…." when you outline the process for check in/out or reservations. Of course, it is important not to use too many words after you just said something was simple! Keep it easy and brief.

4. The Service Shopper – The last segment is the rarest, but this is someone who is looking for something unique for their vacation or likes the feeling of direct access to the owner in order to get the best experience. These guests tend to be verbose in inquiries and emails, but oftentimes will call the owner to speak directly. In some ways, this type of call may feel a bit like an interview. Service shoppers, more than any other group, want to connect with the owner.

How to appeal to Service Shoppers – Service shoppers crave connection, so grant them that access. These conversations don't take a lot of time and having guests who are highly likely to return and care for your property is extremely valuable. Treat them like they are special and your home is a bit of their home. When there is a place you return to with your family many times, it's natural to feel like it's "your place." Often, there is no substitute for knowing the guest can get in touch with you any moment they need to.

Highlighting extra support or features of the rental can also be effective with these guests. Call out 24/7 guest support or extra services such as advance mailing of gate passes are examples that make guests feel important. If you have conversations with a service shopper, share your experiences with the property with them. If they are up for it, this will likely make them feel more a part of the "family."

Making Your Home Appealing to Guests

In order to stand out to guests choosing their vacation spot, it's critical to have a modern looking place. Giving your property a modern look and feel doesn't have to break the bank. However, you may have to make some purchases. Modernization will pay dividends in booking your place and the guest experience post-booking. Here are a few lower-cost items that can make a big difference.

1. Lighting – Modern style light fixtures can really make an impact on a room. I see many property listings with light

fixtures from the 70s/80s. Fixtures that are more modern can be had for $40-$50 each, so pick a few to make a big impact. Upgrading lampshades is another low-cost way to give the room a new look for a cheap price. If you aren't comfortable wiring new light fixtures, just hire an electrician to come in once you have a few to install. I have taken a number of lamps from our home to our vacation properties, which my wife loves, as she can buy some new ones for our full-time house!

2. Bedding – Older style comforters can really date a room. The older they look, the more questions it brings about other aspects of the vacation home. Nobody wants a dated, tired vacation place! New comforter sets that look great can be had for less than $100 and make big impact. Pillows with shams also project and create a luxury feel, so I highly recommend those as well. Buy quality, thick pillows. When time to buy them, high quality comfortable mattresses are very important. Sealy and Stearns & Foster are fantastic options. A pillow top mattress pad can create comfort at low cost. Pinzon makes a great pillow topper available through Amazon I have used on a couple beds. It's a great investment for master beds at $70 each.

Guests will rave about comfortable beds and if you have a name brand mattress, say so in the detail section of the listing. If you have a pillow topper, that's not a bad mention either if you feel that the bed is super comfortable. These details matter! Lastly, a word about blankets. I highly recommend purchasing fleece blankets for each bed. Fleece is soft and gives a luxury feel. In particular, Berkshire makes some of the best blankets out there. If you want to save a bit, get a luxury Berkshire for the master bedroom and order the rest from Target. Target sells some good, soft options. Fleece blankets are easy care and can be cleaned in the washer. For most, sleeping is an important part of the vacation so create some luxury that shows in your pictures but really delivers comfort when your guests arrive. You will also love these items when you vacation there yourself!

3. Wall Art – I have noticed many vacation property listings that have very small and cheap looking pictures on the wall. I am not suggesting buying expensive pictures, but if it looks cheap, get rid of it! No art is better than small, cheap-looking stuff. You can find neat and inexpensive metal wall-art at Amazon or Kirklands.com. Buy a couple bigger pieces for common areas of your home (above a fireplace, or in a family room). Some great designs are available for $60-$70 each. These show up really well in your listing pictures and give guests a modern feel, even when other décor isn't so new.

4. Eliminate Clutter – Both my properties were purchased fully furnished, and it was staggering how much stuff there was crammed into every corner. I hauled truckloads of blankets, pillows, and comforters out of each property and donated it to Goodwill. Clutter is messy and does not project a modern and well-maintained property. Less is more!

A couple more expensive items that can make a big impact:

1. TVs – Flat panel TVs are cheaper than ever and guests really expect them. Buy the largest sizes you can reasonably afford and wall-mount them with cheap mounts from Amazon. Also, invest in a few streaming Blu-ray players if you can. Guests love to stream Netflix (especially if they have kids) and it keeps your movie library from walking off. The convenience can't be beat!

2. Furniture – As we all know, furniture can get expensive fast. Sometimes, though, it's necessary. If you think the furniture in your vacation rental looks like it was bought in the 70s or 80s, so does everyone else. Fortunately, there are more discount furniture options than ever through retailers like Target, Amazon and Walmart. They have modern options that don't have to break the bank. Kitchen tables/chairs, barstools and sofas are all critical to making a modern and clean look.

3. Mattresses – As discussed above, comfortable sleep for you and your guests should be a priority. Mention name brands in your listing and when you create something special for guests, like a plush pillow top, don't be shy mentioning it.

Gold Mining Tips

1. Know who your guests are as they choose property to increase your odds of successfully connecting and booking.

2. Assess your inquiries for signs of one of the four types of vacation shoppers.

3. Give Bargain Shoppers a discount if it is advantageous for you.

4. Load up your listing and website with information (in the right places) for Researchers.

5. Encourage Researchers to ask questions and respond promptly.

6. Promote features that make things easy to Convenience Shoppers.

7. Give Service Shoppers access to you as owner and be highly available.

8. Invest selectively in décor upgrades to modernize the look of your property.

Chapter 5 – Choose Property - Create an Exceptional Listing

"In the world of Internet Customer Service, it's important to remember your competitor is only one mouse click away."

– Doug Warner

Now that you have such an appealing and modern property, show it off in an exceptional listing. If you have spent a great deal of time browsing a listing site, you have likely seen many lackluster listings. When I say lackluster, I don't mean listings that are necessarily bad, but they just don't stand out. The owner or property manager didn't put much thought or time into creating the listing. This is puzzling, since listings aren't cheap and this is your moment to shine! This section of the book will focus on putting your best foot forward to prospective guests to get the most bookings for your marketing dollars.

First, think for a moment about what your prospective guests are looking for as they shop vacation properties. They are dreaming about their vacation, and chances are they get one or two a year at most. Guests are dreaming, because vacations are EXPERIENCES. The vacation rental business is an experience business. Think for a moment about the best vacations you have had. My guess is that you didn't immediately think about a property where you stayed, but instead remembered the time you and your family spent on the beach playing paddleball, or at the theme park laughing hysterically after a roller coaster ride. Even if you did think about the place you stayed when you did that, it was in the context of what you were doing at the time. The best listings draw you into the experience of being there. What will I be doing? What will I be enjoying? What will it be like? Exceptional listings take the guest there and answer these questions. When guests can see enough from your listing to dream about their vacation, you nailed it!

The best at capturing and marketing experience is the Ritz Carlton. Get on their email list so you can see how they sell experiences to their prospective guests. Look at this email example.

Ritz Carlton Email, Accessed 2/19/2014

Notice the crisp, clean look. Next, look at the main picture of the table with nobody sitting there. Wait, that spot is for me, and it looks special. Can you imagine how much my wife would love to have dinner there in that great place for just the two of us? Oh, I can click "Plan Your Stay" to learn more about it and setup a reservation. The best experiential marketers come up with amazingly inviting settings and get you to imagine being there. Next, take a look right below to the "Art of the Craft" section. If you click on this, it takes you to a set of videos about how the

Ritz Carlton creates top-notch experiences for its customers.[6] This is interesting as someone in a small segment of the hospitality industry, but these videos speak volumes on how critical the guest experience is to the Ritz. It tells prospective guests the background of what they are trying to create, and gives them a backstage pass to how they do it.

Well, all of this is very exciting. It's very tempting to jump right in and start writing and uploading pictures. That's what I did when I published my first listing. Needless to say, I redid it multiple times before I got it right. I say I got it right, but I update it regularly with new ideas and better photos. Rushing your listing is a bit like a company not really thinking through their next TV or magazine advertising campaign. There is too much at stake to be haphazard, so take the time to plan it out and be purposeful as you decide how best to showcase your property. We will take it step-by-step. If you already have your listing published, it's never too late to go back and walk through these steps and make updates.

Using the Goldmine Toolkit Listing Planner

Use the Goldmine Toolkit Listing Planner to design your listing. You will notice three main sections of the document: listing description, photos, and listing details. When you completed your marketing plan, you spent time identifying the unique characteristics of your property. Use these and your strengths as important aspects to profile in your listing.

---

[6] "The Ritz Carlton Story – The Art of the Craft",<http://www.ritzcarlton.com/en/LetUsStay/Experiences/ArtofTheCraft.htm > (accessed June 18, 2014)

1. Experiential Paragraph – Thinking of the unique characteristics of your property, come up with some ideas on how they could become experiences. Can guests soak up a great view, enjoying a beverage while the sun goes down? If your property is near activities or attractions, those can work as well. Keep writing until you feel your prospective guests can visualize themselves there.

2. Amenity Paragraph – Then, summarize important and not obvious aspects of your property that you think guests will love. Do you have keyless entry, really nice stuff, or things that make vacationing easy? This paragraph should really tell the prospective guest that you have done a lot to make their vacation great. Keep this paragraph focused on 2-3 main amenities. Remember, renovations are a good thing to cover in this section, which will convey an updated property. If you have a website, which we will cover in the next chapter, include a reference to it in this section. The prospective guest can head to that to really research and see the amenities of the place. Grabbing them off the listing site to your website is ideal to showcase your property. Hopefully, they are hooked! Good candidates for this section include things like keyless entry, no check in process, games/books, or on call property management.

3. Proximity Paragraph – What is near your property that will be great for guests? Being walking distance to attraction and activities is a big plus. If your location is a unique characteristic of your property, then you may want to cover that earlier in the listing description. Are you near

the beach, mountains, restaurant, theme parks, golf, tennis etc.?

4. Summary Paragraph – This paragraph is good for things that didn't rise to the top but seem worthy of mention. Keep it to a couple and tie it all together with letting your guest know that you hope they vacation at your property.

Once you have completed this section, you have decided what to emphasize. Now spend editing time to make it exceptional. Go back through with a critical eye. Is it too long for guests to read? Read it aloud. It's amazing how obvious improvements can be when you hear your writing spoken versus just reading.

Once you feel the listing description is ready, enlist some critics. Ask two or more friends or relatives to read it and give you feedback. Pick someone who has never been to your vacation home before and someone who has. For the person who has never been there, they are your target. The critic who has been there can tell you whether they buy how you portrayed the place and what may be missing. Explain that you really want them to be honest with you, and it won't hurt your feelings. Tell them you would like to get feedback from them on whether they think your listing description makes them want to vacation there. Also, you are interested in feedback on grammar, spelling, length, etc. You should appreciate their feedback overall, but can give them some ideas of what to look out for while they read the description. Ideally, you are sitting with your critic and they can read each paragraph and give you their thoughts as they read through. What does it make them think about? Not everyone will be comfortable editing aloud. I recommend continuing to get feedback until you get, "This is really good."

Planning & Taking Exceptional Pictures

"If the photos aren't sharp, the rest doesn't really matter." - Scott Kelby

Most of your prospective guests haven't been to your property, so your pictures are the obvious spot where they judge whether it's right for them. Many guests spend a significant amount of time deciding. If they are serious about your property, the guest will spend time imagining their vacation there. It's crucial that your property pictures allow them to put themselves there.

I purposefully asked you to write the listing description before photos, because it's the most effective way to make sure the pictures support and match the description well. Before you start choosing pictures, plan out what shots are compelling in just a few steps.

As part of the Listing Planner, you will see the photos section, which has twenty-four spots for photos and a description of what you want your guest to see. VRBO & HomeAway allow this many photos and prioritize properties in the search listings that use all of the photo spots. The goal makes sure you have a solid reason for wanting to include the photo, and allows you to check your pictures against that goal for quality. A photo with the goal of conveying a spacious master bedroom isn't compelling if the actual photo doesn't make the room look big. Take a second to fill out the goal for each one, and you may find yourself making different decisions on which photos to include and which shots are good enough for your listing.

First, review the experiential section of the description and determine what pictures could bring that to life. For example, if you talk about soaking in the sunrise/sunset on the balcony, make sure you have at least one picture of this. In most cases, your best shot of the experience you bring to life in the description should be your main picture for the listing that shows up in the thumbnail. This should really help your prospective guest visualize themselves on their vacation at your place.

Next, go through each amenity and determine whether it makes sense to have a photo for it. In many cases, it may not. Highlighting keyless entry in your listing description is a great convenience, but a photo of your keypad lock isn't very exciting to most guests. Excellent outdoor furniture, new appliances and a whole host of other things are good photo candidates. Also, focus on proximity of the area around your home. Proximity usually creates some good photos for the listings. If your property is near places to play tennis or golf, show a shot or two of that. This will allow guests to continue imagining themselves on vacation. If the setting around your vacation home is beautiful and isn't captured in the experiential photos, add one or two of those.

Lastly, use this basic checklist for some essential pictures:
1. Views from the vacation home
2. Front and back of your vacation home
3. Kitchen
4. All bedrooms
5. Living Room/ Family Room
6. Entryway – foyer, etc. if applicable. This is a good shot to show guests what they will see when they arrive.

Do it yourself photos or go with a pro?

There is no disputing that professional photographers can take better pictures than the rest of us. However, there are some compelling reasons to take your property photos yourself beyond it being less expensive. Taking your own property photos allows showcasing different conditions and seasons, as well as keeping your photos up-to-date with changes to your property. Additionally, no one knows your property as well as the owner. You stand a better chance of being able to capture some great photos with that knowledge. You almost can't go wrong hiring a pro, so if you don't want to deal with photos, head that route and just move forward in the book to the listing details section below. For the "do it yourselfer" crowd, keep on reading.

You need a quality DSLR type camera with a standard and telephoto lens. For the inside shots, I highly recommend an external flash with a diffuser, which allows you to soften the light you are bouncing off the ceiling to brighten the room. Fortunately, DSLR cameras have been on the market for some time and are quite affordable. Amazon also offers some good options for low-cost lenses and external flashes. Check out Neewer for a flash, which at the time of writing can be purchased for an unbelievable $40. Sigma makes a telephoto lens that can be useful for some shots. You can use the lens that came with your DSLR for most, or all of your shots.

I have been asked, "How do you take such great pictures?" The truth is I take mediocre pictures mostly, but I take TONS of them and get lucky once in a while. I highly recommend as you work your way through the photo list, take literally hundreds of photos. Very few of them will be good, but you really improve your odds of getting excellent shots. Every time you go to your property, take your camera. Look for new shots, but also keep shooting shots you already have. Sometimes, you get inspired while shooting, resulting in that perfect shot. Shooting in different light, seasons, and times of the day can create that perfect shot for your listing and website. Each of my websites has about 40 pictures in the photo gallery that took me well over 2000 pictures to get right!

A Few Photo Tips –My first tip is to buy Scott Kelby's Digital photography book series. Scott literally taught me everything I know about photography, which admittedly isn't a lot. Buying a book and spending time reading about photography may not sound very appealing, but it actually isn't as big a deal as it sounds. Scott has written a truly exceptional series of books written in plain English and organized very well. Basically, you can just target the sections you are interested in, or you can read each book and skip things as you go. The chapters below are a good foundation for tips for sharp photos, shooting landscapes for outdoor property/view shots, and how to use your flash for great inside photos.

Volume 1, Chapter 1 – Pro Tips for Getting Really Sharp Photos
Volume 1, Chapter 4 – Shooting Landscapes Like a Pro
Volume 2, Chapter 1 – Using Flash Like a Pro
Volume 3, Chapter 1 – Using Flash Like a Pro Part 2

The entire Kindle version can be purchased for around $35. Scott writes the books as if he is beside you coaching you on how to take good pictures. He doesn't go on and on with boring sections about technical details on aperture, but instead tells you what settings to use on your camera and a sentence or two on why it works. For those of us not looking to become true photographers, this is a great timesaver.

Scott will teach you a lot more about taking great pictures than I can, but here are a few important tips when taking property pictures. Buy a good tripod and use it for all of your pictures. No matter how steady your hands are, the tripod makes certain there is no camera movement to blur your perfect photo. Shoot with your camera low in the room, as if you are shooting from a kneeling position. This lower level shot will make each of your rooms seem bigger. When inside, turn all the lights on in the room you are shooting and aim your slave flash towards the ceiling with the diffuser in place. The diffuser goes over the flash and softens the harsh light. Play around with different flash settings to get the proper amount of light. The proper amount of light makes the room bright but also allows the viewer to see what is outside the window. This is especially important if you have a nice view.

As you planned out the photos for your listing, you will recall including a goal of what you wanted your prospective guest to see. These can be used as your listing captions or at least a starting point to create them. Use the captions to tell the guest what they should see when they look at each photo. Imagine you are showing the pictures to someone sitting next to you.

The Listing Details Can Really Matter – After writing that great description and getting the pictures taken, it's tempting to just get that listing out there without spending time on the details of your listing. It's difficult to know exactly what will be important to guests and how many of them will actually read the "fine print" sections. Rest assured, though, your researchers are all over this section and you want to take every opportunity to let your guests know that you have a great place with great stuff in it.

The following sections are particularly important to guests when making their property selection.

Bedrooms – Let your guests know if you have quality mattresses by using brand names if you have them. Stearns & Foster, Sealy, Serta, and Simmons are recognizable as high quality brands. Also, pillow tops are highly desirable.

Entertainment options in the bedrooms such as TVs and Blu Ray Players are good to include. Some guests like to know which floor the bedrooms are on and information about bathroom access. If each of your bedrooms has its own bath, this can be a big selling point to larger groups.

Bathrooms – Include details on the tub and shower configuration of each bathroom. I highly recommend installing rain showerheads as an inexpensive upgrade for your guests. If you have high-end finishes, such as granite or cultured marble counters, list these prominently.

Kitchen – Guests surely don't want to worry about whether kitchen basics will be at your property, so put their minds at ease by making a solid list of contents. Knowing you have a 12-cup coffeemaker can also help them know what filters to bring. Also, if you have any standout kitchen items with major name brands, don't hesitate to mention those as well. Upgraded appliances and countertops, while visible in your pictures, should also be mentioned in the details.

Outside – Chances are your vacation property has appealing outdoor features that your guests will want to enjoy. Make sure the list of outdoor seating areas are detailed and call out any significant features such as hot tubs, pools, etc.

Guests may be interested in the other amenity sections that VRBO/HomeAway provides so make sure you spend time filling out each thoughtfully. The details shouldn't change much over time, so once you have completed this there is generally little need for updates.

Search Position Matters the Most!
"Sometimes you have to spend money to make money." - Unknown

Now that you have created or tuned up your exceptional listing, make sure your prospective guests can easily find you. This may be the most important concept in this entire book. Search position equates to dollars! If you take nothing else from this book, (which would be quite disappointing) be maniacal about your listing search position.

One of my properties was on VRBO for years before we purchased it, but was in the bottom half to third of the search listings. I changed many things when we purchased the property, but one of the biggest was stepping up Platinum VRBO to get it to the top 10% of listings in the area. In the first year, we brought in three times the rental revenue as the previous owners, which equated about $20,000 more annually. The basic listing on

VRBO was $350 for the prior owner and I bumped that up to $1000 for Platinum. Simply put, the $650 more of marketing spend generated $20k more rental revenue. That's a deal anyone would take all day long. My second property was with a traditional rental company, so the results were even greater. It's important to invest wisely in marketing, but if you do nothing else, buy as much search position as you can possibly afford, where the most prospective guests will see you.

So why does search position matter so much? Your listing needs lots of eyeballs staring at it to generate inquiries, bookings and high rental rates. Here are a few key reasons awesome listing position is so powerful.

1. Listing Traffic Drops off Quickly Down the Property List
More listing views mean more bookings. The sad reality is if your listing is buried in a pile of two thousand in your vacation area, it really doesn't matter how exceptional it is. If no one is seeing it, you won't get many bookings.

When I first started with a Platinum VRBO listing, I also had an entry-level HomeAway listing on one of my properties for a year. I booked forty-five weeks that year (we used four weeks ourselves), but only one of those weeks was booked from HomeAway. My listing was completely buried and no one was seeing it. Just like the quote at the beginning of the book pointed out, I was winking at a girl in a dark room.

Many studies have been done on search position and traffic through Google that can be generalized to vacation listing sites. According to a 2013 study by online ad network

Chitika[7], the first page of Google search results get 91.5% of the click through traffic and the second page gets 4.8%. Given that equates to the top ten results, this is a telling statistic. It says we all have short attention spans when it comes to online research.

To further reinforce this point, the study states that the top search result gets 33% of the click through traffic while the second gets 10%. From there the traffic drops off quickly. There are certainly differences between general Google searches and vacation listing sites; however, online shopping behavior through both likely has consistent themes. Since the top two spots are hard to get, the hope is that prospective guests will search harder for something as important as their vacation. As you saw above, if your guest gets to the second page, the click-through rates drop off dramatically.

More listing views mean more money. Maniacally focus on your search position and make it your quest to make it the best it can be! Help your guests find your great place for their vacation.

2. Higher Rental Rates in Peak Season

Typically, renting in the peak season isn't too difficult. Maximizing your rental income is more than just getting the place rented. Your goal is to provide your guests a great value, while putting the most dollars in your pocket. Your odds of getting top dollar for your property go way up when you have lots of guests shopping your listing. Greater guest

---

[7] Chitika, "The Value of Google Result Positioning," June 7, 2013, <http://chitika.com/google-positioning-value> (accessed June 18, 2014).

views could also mean finding just the right sized party to divvy up the rent, or a smaller party that doesn't worry much about cost.

When you are way up in the search results for your destination, you also get a lot of advance shoppers and tend to book up significantly earlier than those properties further down the list. Being really booked is a great way to get additional bookings. Guests will view your property as highly desirable, and will often be willing to pay more for it. In that way, booking success begets success.

Get top dollar in the busy season by getting lots of shoppers and early bookings.

3.   Booking the Off-Season
The number of guests shopping for off-season vacations goes WAY down in most vacation locales. Owners have to try harder to get bookings. Getting fully booked in the off-season is one of the strongest moves you can make towards maximizing rental income. When the guest shopping traffic goes way down, you can't afford to be way down in the heap, or guests won't find you. With a nearly limitless supply, they just won't get to your listing. Step up in search position and grab those elusive off-season bookings.

4.   Attracting Last Minute Travelers
Last minute travelers don't typically have time to shop extensively for a vacation property. They instead go looking for something available that can meet their needs for a quick

getaway. If you have good search position, these folks will quickly get to your listing, and when they like what they see, they will book for their fast-approaching vacation. This is a great way to get some off-season bookings.

5. Getting the Most from Listing Site & Email Marketing
Listing sites tend to do lots of marketing to drive traffic to their site. This can benefit you if your locale happens to be one of the featured destinations. Better search position means this generated traffic will be much more likely to find you. If your locale gets an email campaign, it can be extremely powerful.

A couple years ago while I was at work, I noticed I was receiving one inquiry after the next. I received forty-four inquiries that day for all kinds of vacation timeframes, and it literally took me hours to respond to them all. I found out the listing site had picked my vacation property to be one of those profiled in an email campaign. My listing page received thousands of views that day. I feel certain they picked my place largely because I was easy to find. If you are way up in the search results, guests responding to this marketing will see you quickly and will hopefully jump on an inquiry or booking.

Obsess About Your Listing Search Position
The first step is to develop a good understanding of how your listing site determines search position. Like Google, most listing sites won't tell you exactly how this works, but will give you a general idea. Read what you can online, but I also suggest calling your listing site provider to discuss this topic and ask lots of questions. Tell them you are interested in improving your search

position and need their help to figure out what you can do. Keep trying things with their guidance until you run out of things to do. I also suggest calling multiple times to speak to a few different agents about this topic, as they may give you additional or different guidance. You can take a break when you hear multiple agents say that there is nothing more you can do to move your listing up.

For VRBO/HomeAway, a few significantly important factors determine search position at the time of writing:

1. Buy the Highest Tier Listing – It's not the listing cost that matters, it's the return that's important. While it costs a few hundred dollars more to buy a top tier listing, it typically only takes one more rental to pay for the increase. From there, incremental rental income goes to the bottom line. HomeAway fairly recently launched their US bundle: $250 gets you the same tier listing on their sister site. So if you have a Platinum VRBO listing, then the bundle gets you Platinum on HomeAway. This is a great deal, especially given the large cost of buying both listings separately. Both sites are fantastic rental producers for my properties. Bumping up the search position has produced thousands more dollars of rental income and has made it easier for my guests to find my property. We are talking real money here!

2. Accept HomeAway Payments – HomeAway states they strive to bring the highest quality experience to its users. They feel that listings that accept credit cards make things easier and more convenient for guests. I am happy to

have a high quality payment service for my guests, as I used to rely on a rental company for payments. I have heard from a number of my guests they appreciate being able to easily pay online with their credit card. Credit card payment is an expectation of most guests anyway. Set this up for your guests using HomeAway payments, and you will be rewarded with better listing visibility.

3. Setup Online Bookings (Book It Now) – HomeAway has created a quality set of reservation tools and gives top billing inside the Platinum, Gold, Classic, etc. tiers to listings with "Book It Now" enabled. This means that all rates and rental agreement are setup in the HomeAway listing to allow guests to book themselves. It really depends on the guest as to whether they prefer just to book or whether they would like to send an inquiry and exchange some emails before making a reservation. Owners may worry about losing control of the rental calendar with online bookings; however, the owner is always in control of whether the booking is accepted. This is a big step towards making it easy for your guests to book your vacation. HomeAway rewards listings with Book It Now by propelling them toward the top of their listing tiers. It's good for owners too, as by the time you hear from your prospective guest you may already have their booking!

4. Get as Many Exceptional Guest Reviews as Possible – Your previous guests play a big role in helping future guests feel confident they are making the right vacation property decision. Chapter 10 gets into strategics to

harvest the best reviews from your guests. In addition to helping guest confidence, more five-star reviews propel your listing to a higher search position.

5. Pay Attention to the Listing Dashboard – If you list on HomeAway/VRBO, the listing dashboard provides great information on how they view your listing for search position. HomeAway calls the measure Listing Completeness. A higher Completeness percentage translates into better search position. The rationale, of course, is that listings that are more complete are better for prospective guests, and thus should get higher placement on the site. The Listing Completeness measure is a great place to start with their customer service agents as you discuss how to bump up your search position. They should be able to make suggestions to move the needle.

6. Read Every Word of Email Sent By Your Listing Site – Listing sites tweak, or in some cases overhaul, their search algorithms from time to time. They will typically communicate these changes in advance to their owners. Good listing sites will give you tips to boost your search position. They will also tell you how they are changing algorithms and why. Pay attention to what they tell you and call customer service if you have questions.

While search position on listing sites doesn't typically change a lot, check your search position regularly to make sure you are as close as possible to the top. Other owners may be raising their game, which could push you down the rankings. Great search position by itself won't maximize your rental income, but without it, you are almost certain to leave money on the table. Make it easy for guests to find you and make more money from your vacation property.

Gold Mining Tips

1. Make a list of vacation experiences and pick the best for listing and pictures.
2. Use the Goldmine Listing Planner to outline experiential, amenity, proximity and summary sections.
3. Have multiple critics read your listing and provide feedback.
4. Use your listing text to plan your photos.
5. Take countless photos of each shot and read Scott Kelby's book to improve your photography skills.
6. Buy the best listing position you can afford to get higher rates and more off-season bookings.
7. Learn the details on how your listing site determines search position and do what they reward to get the best position.
8. Check your listing position regularly to insure it remains the best it can be.

Chapter 6 – Create a Great Vacation Property Website

"Your website was so much more than one gets on a listing site. The website is what helped us decide on your vacation property."

– Voice of the Guest

N ow that you have an exceptional listing, pair it with a great website that allows your guests to really explore your vacation property. A professional-looking and well-designed website gives you credibility with guests and allows them to get a sense of what their vacation experience will be like.

Why Create a Vacation Property Website?

Credibility with Guests – A professional-looking website makes you look like just that, "a professional." A great URL, such as www.awesomevacationrental.com, can be used on all of your guest communications and give your guests some peace of mind that you are a serious businessperson. Just make sure to substitute your vacation destination for the word awesome above in the URL.

Draw Guests In To Their Vacation – Unlike your listing site(s), a website has a flexible format and can have great visual impact on your guests. A great vacation property website uses huge, high-resolution pictures on the landing page and in the photo gallery to give guests a good sense of what their vacation there will be like.

68

Allow Guests to Research – Give guests lots of information on the site covering details that they may want to research before making a booking decision. Floor plans and area maps are good examples of information that will appeal to many guests who really want to dig into the details about your place.

Connect With Your Guests – While listing sites give you a small spot to share a bit about yourself and why your place is special to you, a website allows you to dedicate an entire page to it. Tell your guests about the vacation experience you strive to create for them. Share some information about yourself and what you do at your home when you are on vacation. Invite them into your future plans for the place, so they can feel ownership in the place with you.

Close the Booking – Your website is your closer, meaning it helps you close the sale. Your guest got interested enough in your listing to click through to your website. The website should be compelling enough to leave no doubt in their mind that your place is where they want to be. All the jaw dropping pictures, professional looking design and vacation home details should give your guests the sense that you have thought of everything and do it all right. Once they see all that, it's time to book!

What Should Guests Get From Your Website?

The key to a great website is a clean and well thought out design. Using the simple design in the Vacation Rental Goldmine Toolkit, think through each guest segment as you plan your content and what they need from the website. The Homepage Design Worksheet and All Other Pages Design Worksheet step you through the process.

The Bargain Shopper wants a deal, and likely won't spend a lot of time on your website except possibly to determine whether they like your place. Big visual impact on the homepage is likely the key. The pricing on your website typically won't be different than your listing site, so the Bargain Shopper is likely to cut to the chase quickly to get a deal. Unlike the Bargain Shopper, the Researcher will spend lots of time on your website accumulating information. The extra-large gallery pictures and details really help researchers get comfortable and make sure they are getting exactly what they want for their vacation. The convenience shopper wants everything to be easy, so clean website navigation and lots of references to convenient features like no check in and out, keyless entry, and mailing vacation documents in advance are good content options. The service shopper wants owner access and a top tier experience. Use website content to let them get to know you. Easy access to your contact info, as well as rich testimonials, is good content. For the testimonials, provide service shoppers quotes from prior guests talking about how accessible and friendly you are, or how much better their experience was with their rental with you than with others. Also, if you have onsite property management or concierge service, these are features custom made for this segment.

An Amateurish Website is Worse than No Website

Most vacation rental books I have read do a great disservice to readers by oversimplifying the property website topic. Some authors make offhand comments about creating your own website being like creating a Microsoft Word document. There are certainly a lot of great website builders out that have brought website creation into reach for the non-techie types. The Vacation Rental Goldmine Toolkit uses WordPress™ to walk you through each step of the process. Knowing how to type a word document does not get you a website. We will put the right tools in your hands to build and maintain your own vacation home website the right way.

Since it's not easy to build a great website, there are a number of "dinky" do-it-yourself looking sites out there. I bet you have seen some that have a couple static pages with lots of text, small pictures, and no flash or dynamic content whatsoever. If you create an amateur website, it makes you and your property look amateur. You want a site that communicates to guests that you and your property are top of the line. A basic or cluttered website won't build credibility or interest in your property.

Since you bought this book, I hope you will invest time to build a great property website, or decide to build no website at all. The step-by-step process in the Goldmine Toolkit gives you the tools and instructions to make it easy. Please invest in a great website because there is no better venue for your property to shine!

Simple Websites Win!

Great websites are simple and clean. In hospitality, Ritz sets the gold standard for websites as well. Studying their site is a great help before digging in to design your own.

www.ritzcarlton.com, Accessed 8/28/14

The page has huge visual impact, mostly due to the incredible resort paradise picture on the Slider. A Slider rotates content on the page. This photo slider displays five high-impact photos in sequence and really draws you into the vacation experience. The clean and crisp design is immediately noticeable. The page uses contrasting content and white space to increase visual appeal.

Clear navigation makes things easy for visitors, and the Ritz page does this very elegantly using a top navigation bar. They have likely found many of their visitors come to search and make reservations, so that capability is prominent on the home page. While the page is far from crowded, experiential content abounds on the page with the big photo, a section on memories, and the lower section is about marriage proposal. They cover a bit of vacation everything on this page with very few words.

www.ritzcarlton.com/en/Promotions/Offers/AllOffers.htm
Accessed 8/28/14

The Offers page employs many of the homepage design concepts. It mirrors the top navigation and features a high impact banner photo. The pictures and text clearly show the guest what it's like to be there. Reading through the offers, the Ritz uses "you" references to draw guests into the experience. The page design is straightforward, yielding a quick and informative read. This simple website is great!

How to Design Your Vacation Property Website

Professional web design firms make millions creating website designs. I am going to teach you some of their tricks so you can easily design and build a great vacation rental website of your own. There are many good website building tools out in the marketplace. WordPress™ has powerful website creation and search engine optimization capabilities. It was created as a blogging tool, but evolved into a full web authoring solution. WordPress™ uses themes to create the website format. In the Goldmine Toolkit, we will use a Theme called Travelify, which captures many of the excellent design characteristics of the Ritz site.

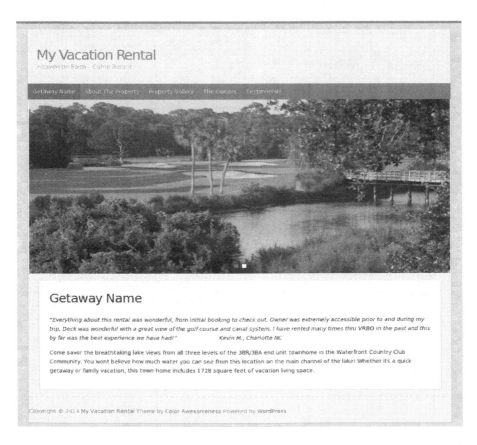

This is a sample vacation rental homepage I quickly created using WordPress™. The step-by-step instructions to do this are included in the toolkit. A number of the design components are similar to the Ritz page. It has a huge photo slider for your very best photos to draw guests into the vacation experience. It also employs a simple top navigation bar. The bottom section of the page can be formatted in a variety of ways and is as simple to modify as a word document. Like the Ritz homepage, this page is simple and great!

Create a Homepage Sketch

In the web design world, designers create a sketch of each page called a wireframe. A wireframe captures the layout of the pages. Using the WordPress™ Travelify theme, the layout is already setup for you; the content is 100% up to you. It's important to do an outline to plan all of the content before you start building pages in WordPress™. Once you sit down to start the step-by-step instructions, you have already figured out what content is going where, which really speeds things along.

The Goldmine Toolkit has two worksheets that you can use for your sketches, setup with the layout of the pages you are going to build. Start out with the Homepage Design Worksheet. There are just a few simple steps to sketch out the homepage. I recommend printing out the worksheet and using a pencil to sketch things out. You will note that the steps below correspond directly to the worksheet sections. While important to put some thought into this, I bet you can sketch this page out in about twenty minutes. Let's get started!

Step 1 – Dream Up Your Page Title
The page title should be the brand you have decided on for your site. This could be the address of your home if you have a catchy street name, such as "123 Beach Drive."

Step 2 – Pick a Subtitle
The subtitle should just be a few descriptive words about your vacation home. Something like "A Waterfront Paradise" or "Luxury Mountain Getaway" are examples that could work well. See if you can describe your vacation home in three to four words.

Step 3 – Decide On Site Pages for Top Navigation Bar
Determine what pages you want to have on your site and list the names across the top navigation bar. Keep the page names simple, using just one or two words for each. Consider the following pages for your Vacation Rental Site, but of course, the beauty of your own website is that you can build whatever pages you want! Common pages include Property Details, Gallery, Calendar, Testimonials, and Owners.

Step 4 – Pick the Pictures for your Photo Slider
Go through your property pictures and pick your 4-5 clearest and most eye popping pictures of the views, home, or surroundings. The Ritz Carlton site was a great example to follow, as their slider shots are crisp, clear, experiential and just generally inviting. Inside shots are generally less interesting for this spot unless you have an impressive and newly renovated interior. If your home could be profiled on the Houzz website, then by all means, please highlight the interior on the homepage. If you haven't been to Houzz, it's a fantastic website of photos showing ideas for any

home. Features such as decks or patios are excellent experiential choices.

Step 5 – Write Text for Bottom Section

A guest testimonial is a highly effective way to lead off the page footer or bottom page section. Good testimonial candidates include general comments about how incredible the guest experience was. This is particularly true if the guest compares your place favorably to others. If you don't have a standout general testimonial, go searching for one that highlights what you decided to show on the page in your slider. Your Marketing Plan highlights the feature(s) that standout for your property. The key feature should be prominent in the photo slider and testimonial. The voices of your guests speak with much greater volume than anything you say, so make the most of these gems.

With the remainder of the footer, write a few short sentences on an experience that is evident in the photo slider. Whether you have a beach, mountain, or city home there should be no shortage of options. Pick one or two for a few short sentences on the homepage. Many visitors may not read this section, and those who do aren't likely to stay long. Draw them in quickly.

Finish the bottom contact information section to make it easy for guests to get in touch with you.

Sketching Out the Other Webpages

The homepage is the toughest to sketch out, because you made many overall site decisions. Use the All Other Pages Design Worksheet and Gallery Design Worksheet to step through each of the subsequent pages. The body of the page is the only content that is changing from page to page, so this should go quickly. The most time-consuming part will likely be writing the text for the property and owner pages and picking the photos for the gallery.

Property – Include a great picture of the front of your place. Then create experiential text about what it's like to be there. Highlight some of the unique and great features you identified in your marketing plan. Include a floor plan if you have it or can draw it. The property page can have some of the same text as your listing, but make certain to include new information as well.

Gallery – This is your opportunity to put as many pictures on the site as you want. While you could go wild with pictures, make sure you have a guest-focused purpose for each picture. What do you want them to see and why? If you can answer that question and feel good about it, then add the picture. Use the Gallery Design Worksheet to make a list of the pictures along with the captions and order to show them. The order is quite important, so make sure to prioritize your pictures as well. As cool as you think the pictures are, most visitors to your site won't stick around to see your entire slide show. A Researcher might watch it all the way through multiple times, but your average visitor is likely to hang in there for 10-15 pictures at best. Make those first ten really count, and include a nice mix of outside and inside pictures. It's ok to use some of the same pictures you have on your listing, as the gallery gives bigger views that should allow guests to see more detail. Add some extra photos of the surrounding area and activities that can help your guests visualize their vacation.

Owners – I highly recommend you include an Owners page. Rent-by-owner guests generally like to connect with the owners in some way and feel like they are guests in their home. This differentiates the vacation home rental market from more of a hotel arrangement. What better way to make the home and experience seem special than to add some story to the experience and allow your guests to connect to you.

There are three important things to accomplish on the owner page.

1. Share a bit about you and your family with your guests. Some of your guests won't care much, but others will. Often, your prospective guest is female and women are most likely to appreciate a personal connection. To continue my rampant overgeneralization, men typically aren't as much into personal connection, but may find it interesting nonetheless. A friendly looking picture of you, with or without your family, may provide your guests the feeling that it will be easy to work with you. Perhaps they even feel an allegiance with you, as you could be similar in some way. Share a bit of yourself and you may be surprised how often guests will use the information to strike up a conversation with you. It's neat for everyone, in my opinion.

2. Tell your guests why your vacation is special to you and your family. Perhaps you vacationed in the area for years and knew a place for you was the logical next step. You may be planning to retire there one day. In short, tell your guest the story of your love affair with the place. How

often do you come there? What do you do when you go there? What do you love about it?

3. Tell your guests about the experience you strive to create for them while on vacation. Vacation is a big deal and sizeable expenditure. By implementing this book, you are going to great lengths to make sure your guests are getting fantastic experiences. Make sure you tell them this. They may get the idea by seeing convenient features and on-site support, but don't leave it to chance. If you feel passion for your guests, they need to know it! Revisit this section of the Owners page once you complete the book and keep striving to put it into words for your guests. Use your own words, but here is an excerpt from my Owners page to get you started.

One important thing to mention is the level of service we intend to provide our guests. A vacation is a big deal, and unfortunately, most of us don't get to go on one very often. Things need to be right; you should have all the comforts of home, and you shouldn't have to spend a lot of time on logistics of picking up keys and other things that rob your vacation time. This should be relaxing and fun. We have added a number of amenities to the villa in an effort to create this experience for you - keyless entry to the villa and brand new technology all around to make the experience even more convenient and fun. When you rent the villa, you receive a detailed amenity sheet with instructions so you can get the most from your vacation experience. We have a local company that is there for you as well should you need something. I am always available via phone or email, but the local presence is critical to your experience. We want you to have the best time ever and come back again and again!

Key messages in the above are that vacations and our guests are a big deal. We work to make it great for guests so they come back again and again. Play around with this until you feel like you have something genuine that captures it in your own words.

Rates – A simple rate page is good to have just in case your guest arrives at your site without going to the listing site. Keep the page simple and easy to read. Information on this page should generally be limited to seasonal rate information, a few important policies, and an offer to put together a custom quote for the guest. Seasonal rate information is straightforward, but break down the weekly, nightly, and monthly rates as applicable. Policies may include things like deposit schedule, rental age limits, pet policies, limits to number of guests, refundable security deposit etc. Keep this section to just a few of the most important policies at this stage and save the bulk of these for your rental agreement. List only the rules that you think could be important to their decision-making process. You don't want to seem overly rigid or unfriendly to your guests by throwing a bunch of rules in their face. For example, don't bother listing a rule against parties on this page. Most of your guests aren't going on vacation to throw a big party and generally understand that vacation places have rules against them. Absolutely cover this rule in your rental agreement and your guests can ask you about it if they have concerns. Too many rules at this stage can give your guests the wrong idea about what it's like to work with you.

Testimonials – Once you have been renting your home for a while, you should be accumulating guest testimonials. As a rule, vacations are great, and it shouldn't be too difficult to come up with great things to say about them. If you are truly investing in creating great guest experiences, you should get glowing feedback with ease. It is important to ask for testimonials, which we will cover more in a future chapter. There is little more powerful to prospective guests than the words of guests who have come before them. List them out with the best ones first. Like anything on your website, it's rare that folks will sift through them all, so pick the first three or four very carefully.

If your guests feel particularly compelled, they may give you very long testimonials, which are a great thing. Since you know most of your visitors may not read for very long, it may be good to take excerpts of their testimonials so your guests can get through a number of them quickly. Some testimonials will shine above all the others. When guests say they had their "best vacation ever" or your place is "the best yet," well you can't beat those with anything else. Send them to the top of the heap on your testimonials page. The second big grouping is any testimonial that brings your key differentiator to life. When your guests notice and rave about what makes your place different, that is also something to broadcast loudly to prospective guests. The third type to emphasize on the list is any testimonials that mention how great you are to work with as the owner. Where you have made the guest's time special, this can really demonstrate that you will deliver a top-notch vacation experience for them. A great variety of testimonials can give guests their choosing of what they want to read about to make them secure about their vacation.

The Importance of a Good URL

At this point, you have sketched out each page, know what copy or text to include, and which photos you plan to use. The next *log cabin getaway   log Cabin Vacation   Cabin Vacation   Cabin getaway   log home Vacation   Country getaway*

thing to decide when you are getting setup is what URL you will use for your homepage. URL stands for Uniform Resource Locator and is the "www.yourawesomevacationrental.com" for your website. What to substitute for "yourawesomevacationrental.com" is an important decision and one to spend some time thinking about and researching. You want your URL to project your site as a big deal and easy to remember. You will add this URL to all of your guest communications, so make it good. *lagrange log Cabin*

In addition to being easy to remember, consider how guests Google search for vacation rental options in your area. It's unlikely you will be able to compete with the big listing sites for traffic, but in some locales, you may have a chance. Choose a URL closely related to how guests think about searching in your area. This may lead them to the conclusion that your site and property are prominent in the area and worthy of consideration. Also, this could make it more likely that they could remember your site address for the future. While some folks claim to understand how Google Search works, very few folks actually do. If your URL contains search terms, it's reasonable to believe that Google may pay attention to that in their search results. It won't be a big factor to get better search position, but it can't hurt.

Navigate to Bluehost.com or Godaddy.com to play around with search terms and see what's available as a URL. If your home is in a major vacation destination area, creativity may be required to find something good. Another option could be to focus on the resort name where your place resides to lock in a good URL. URLs with the word "vacation" and "rental" are effective. Given that you are unlikely to place well in Google search, focus instead on something easy for guests to remember. Once you decide on the URL, reserve it with whatever Internet Service Provider (ISP) you plan to host the site with. The step-by-step Website Building Instructions use Bluehost, so follow them to get the URL if you plan to build the site there.

Building the Site

There are many excellent site builders in the marketplace. The webpage sketches you made earlier in this chapter fit well with the Travelify WordPress™ Theme. Whether you ultimately decide to purchase the Goldmine Toolkit including the step-by-step instructions, I highly recommend WordPress™ to build your site. Bluehost is a great low cost hosting solution with excellent instructions on getting a Wordpress™ site built. The Goldmine Create Property Website instructions eliminates the hours of research and guesswork by taking you click by click through building your Vacation Property Website. If you aren't technical and have limited time, I highly recommend using the instructions as a major saver.

With the tough decisions of what to include made, building the site will be largely mechanical. Pay close attention as you build though, so you have a good idea how to maintain the site for changes and updates. Maintaining your own site is so much better than having to pay someone every time you want to do something online. You have the keys!

I highly recommend purchasing a WordPress™ book to help with the build and maintenance. A book is not required, as the click-by-click instructions walk you through everything; however, if you decide to do something different or new with your site the book can be a big help. Also, you might get stuck on a particular step and the book may provide information that's helpful. Just send me an email if you are stuck, and I am happy to help. *Teach Yourself Visually WordPress*™ by Janet Majure is a strong basic book on WordPress™ that gets high marks from me based on all of the click-by-click screenshots that make it easy to follow. You can pick up the Kindle version or a used copy for about $5 at the time of writing. A small price to pay versus getting a pro to help with your site for updates or new pages.

Making Sure You Have a Great Site

Companies spend millions in their quest for a great website. You put a lot into planning and making your site and surely you want it to be good. In the industry, this is typically done through user research, where everyday folks review and react to web pages. Research firms make good money getting feedback for businesses, but you can do it for free or super cheap.

First, we will start with the free route. Have a few friends or family members review your site with you sitting by their side. The less computer-savvy they are, the better. Ask them to view the site as if they were considering renting your place and to the extent they feel comfortable talk about their impressions as they navigate. An impression, meaning what stands out to them, or thoughts they have, while looking through it. Don't ask them any questions during this, but instead take notes on what they say as they explore the site noting the page and comment. Asking them questions or otherwise talking to them may distract them or lead them in a direction that's different from what they might naturally do. Watch where they go, and in what order. Since you have Google Analytics™ on your site, you can go back later and determine how much time they spent in specific spots. This will be longer than average, because they are talking and being more thorough than your typical guest will be.

After your reviewer does a freeform walk through the website, ask them questions:

What are your general impressions looking at the site?

Was it in plain English and easy to find what you were looking for?

Which pictures were most useful? Could some be better? Were any missing?

What pages were the best and why?

What would make the site better?

Do this with three or more reviewers if you can. As the website author, you are too close to the site and content to be objective. You will likely get a number of good ideas to make the site better. Go back through your notes and highlight the changes you plan to implement.

Another way to do site research is to hire a web usability professional on Fiverr.com to review your site. Many of these folks will do these reviews for $5 and send you a report or video with feedback. Research the reviews from the seller to make sure their prior customers have been happy with the end product, because many may claim to be usability experts. I used a Fiverr service and received some good suggestions to implement on my sites. Some sellers on Fiverr will even run a small focus group for you and send you feedback. That is a small price to pay for feedback that could take you to more bookings!

Getting Found Online

Now that your website is built, how will your guests find you? Keeping in mind your website's primary goal is to be your "closer" for bookings, the most urgent thing to do is to get your listings linked up to it. Chances are your listings and your guest communications will be the primary traffic drivers. If you are listing on VRBO, log into your dashboard and add the link by going to Edit Listing and putting the link entry on the Links and Video Tab.

SEO stands for Search Engine Optimization and is a very important component to your website being found. SEO is about getting the best search position with search engines like Google and Bing. Search engines have programs called robots that continually work to index the internet. SEO is the "science" that makes sure the crawlers know what your site is about and will return it early in the search. Search engine algorithms change frequently and are quite mysterious, as no one really knows how they work. WordPress™ does the SEO tagging for you, so you don't even need to worry about it once you know what you want to do. If you want to go deep on SEO, I would recommend hiring someone unless you are a major technology nerd or aspire to be one.

Google and other search engines are highly motivated to put the best content first in their search results. They have built their business on relevancy as bringing the right content brings visitors to their site to search. Having many visitors translates into advertising revenue from big companies and that makes Google money. So how does Google decide what good content is?

You may have figured out while you were using WordPress™ that it is actually building the code for your webpages behind the scenes. While doing that, it's generating keywords and description information based on what you are putting on each page. Search engines use these keywords and descriptions to know what your site is about. The search engines have robots that crawl and index the web so that when anyone enters keywords on Google.com, Google knows what webpages to bring back in what order. In recent years, search engines have become more sophisticated in how they determine best content by prioritizing things like how often other sites link to a site. Search engines also highly prioritize social media such as Pinterest and Facebook. The idea being that if the world of the internet thinks a site is good enough to talk about or link to, other visitors will like it. Makes sense when you think about it. I could say many awesome things about my site, but that doesn't make it good. Visitors coming to it speaks much more to whether it's good than anything I can say about it.

You could spend countless hours getting backlinks setup and building Facebook and Pinterest sites, but I argue that this will likely get you minimal results. Top listing sites have invested big here and already lock up the top Google spots. You won't be able to compete with them. Just consider that part of what you are paying for from your listing fee, and focus your time and energy elsewhere. Instead, make sure your website content and the rest of your guest experience is great. That will get you much more in results than the mysterious world of SEO ever will.

The other way to be found is to display your URL in prominent places in guest communication. Add it to the email signature you use to communicate with guests. If that is the same email you use for other communications, your friends will likely see it too. That way, they can mention it to other friends. Other places to make it prominent are in inquiry responses and thank you postcards, which we will cover in later chapters.

Keeping In Touch With the Online Guest Experience

Now that your site is being traveled by guests, you can get some good information about what they are doing while there and how well it's working. If you followed the click-by-click build instructions, you hopefully have Google Analytics™ working on your site now. This is the best tool to keep an eye on your website experience. Some key questions to answer:

1. How many guests are coming to my website?
2. How are they finding me online?
3. What geographic areas are most of my guests coming from?
4. What are guests doing on my site
5. Is it working well for them?

www.google.com/analytics/, Accessed 8/28/14

Knowing guest visitor volumes and how they found you can provide comfort knowing your site is being used. If, for example, you notice you aren't getting traffic from VBRO or Homeaway.com, it may be useful to check the link is still on the listing. You could also refer to the link in the description section to direct folks to it for additional volume. Visitor volumes can be found on the main dashboard and traffic source under Acquisition and All Traffic. All Traffic shows you how much traffic you are getting from each site – Google, Direct Traffic via Link or URL entry, VRBO referrals, etc.

Analytics also provides data about where your guests are located. How is that more than just a point of interest? When you receive guest inquiries, you often get a contact phone number that can give you an idea where the guest lives. You can track that through the Geo Tab to Location to see if the guest has visited your website. Assuming they came to the site, knowing whether they spent a lot of time there or not can tell you how interested they are in renting it. Clearly, this isn't a perfect measure of interest as they may have already decided they want to book and therefore just gave it a quick look. Where this comes in particularly handy is when you are trying to decide whether to offer an off-season discount. If the guest seems to have a high degree of interest, offering a smaller discount may make them very happy. Conversely, the guest breezing through the site may tell you they are looking at lots of options and the discount should be sweeter.

Analytics gives lots of great data on the site, but the most important section of all is the Behavior and Flow. Engagement online is generally measured by how long a visitor stays on the site and how much they explore while there. The Behavior tab of Google Analytics™ focuses here and is a great source of information about how useful your site is for your guests. Guests on average should stay on your site for multiple minutes. You will see some who perhaps landed there by mistake, but you have content on your pages that should take a couple minutes to consume. As you look at this data, you can learn some very interesting things about how the site is working for your guests.

Look first at the average amount of time your guests are spending on the site. If after a few hundred visitors, you find they aren't staying for at least a couple of minutes, your site may not be grabbing them on the main page. You can view these on the Overview tab of the Behavior section. This will also tell you volumes on each of your other pages as well. Having uniform volume across all your pages is a good thing, which shows your guests find your pages interesting enough to at least view them. The Content Drilldown option on Analytics lets you see how long guests are staying on each page. Your Property Details and Gallery pages are likely to hold your guests attention longer due to rich information and great pictures. If guests aren't spending significant time with your gallery, possibly it isn't working properly, or more likely, they aren't seeing pictures that keep them looking. Time how long it takes for the pictures to make a complete cycle and use that as a gauge of how long guests stay. The Behavior Flow option also can be useful as it shows you the page-to-page movement of your guests. On my sites, guests tend to go from the Homepage to Property Details and then to the Gallery. If there is something very important that you want your guests to know, tell them on a page early in the flow. This section tells you about drop offs as well, when guests leave the site. They may have all the information they need or just lose interest. It's good to look for trends in all this data to make sure guests look to be getting what they need.

A Word or Two about Social Media

I would be remiss not to mention social media, but this book doesn't spend time covering it. Some owners have done neat things with Facebook pages, but it can be a lot of work to do well. Content is king in social media and you need to have something to post on a regular basis to have a quality Facebook presence. I can't think of what I would post about my place on a regular basis that folks would find interesting. Pinterest boards have popped up some places on vacation destinations, and they require less care and feeding. If you are highly creative or already big into Facebook, please don't let me discourage you. When done well, Google rewards social media very highly so it can be a great traffic generator. For me, I don't see a big payback on the time investment and instead focus elsewhere.

Congratulations on setting up a great web presence! It's sure to deliver by getting you more bookings as your "closer."

Gold Mining Tips

1. Continue the experiential theme from your listing to your website.
2. Focus on simple design and create sketches of each page.
3. Use the website to showcase everything that's great about your property, which includes you!
4. Pick a URL that contains search words for your destination.
5. Use the Goldmine Toolkit Website Instructions for a step-by-step build of the website.
6. Have some critics go through your site and provide real time feedback. Also consider hiring a website reviewer on fiverr.com.
7. Install Google Analytics to see what your guests are doing on the site and the source/volume of traffic.

Chapter 7 – Choose Property – Vacation Property Comparison Shopping

"I don't feel bad about online shopping at work. It's the only place where I can spend money WHILE I make it."

—Unknown

T he guest has browsed your listing and possibly your website and they like what they see! So, they send you an inquiry. Now that you have their attention, what's next? How can you make your property stand out and get this guest to come stay at your fantastic vacation home?

Characteristics of Great Inquiry Responses

Your guest is interested, and this is another opportunity to market your great vacation home to them. Here are a few characteristics of standout inquiry responses:

1. Visually Appealing & Compelling – Your response should look professional and take your guest on vacation. HTML email makes it easier than ever to include beautiful pictures of the vacation setting to remind your guest of why they sent you an inquiry in the first place. Big visual impact means your response will stand out among the masses, before your guest reads a word of content.

2. Concise yet Informative – Strike the right balance of information so your response is read. You get one shot at this, and having something too short or too long may have your guest moving onto other responses. Make it easy for your guests to get the information they need and don't include extra info that is unlikely to affect their booking decision.

3. Welcoming to Your Guest – The inquiry response should communicate that you would love the guest to vacation at your home. Welcome them to make your home their "Home away from home." Also encourage their questions to make them comfortable during the shopping process and ultimately with their booking decision.

4. Friendly & Flexible – Be friendly in your response, giving your guest the feeling you will be easy to work with. As the sales adage goes, "people buy from people they like."

Guests who provide information about themselves, their families, or what they plan to do on vacation are generally great candidates to connect with more personally in the response. Share in their vacation enthusiasm. After all, I bet you are enthusiastic about trips to your vacation home. Flexibility is best demonstrated through answers to your guest's questions. Many things can be worked out through negotiation, so where possible provide options. Also, don't include points in your response where you are flexible unless you think they are essential to your guest's booking decision. For example, I don't include a deposit percentage because I am flexible to work with guests on the percentage they need to confirm their reservation.

Use these characteristics to judge your inquiry response or the one included in the Goldmine Toolkit. Since your inquiry responses will often vary with your guests, keep these factors in mind while crafting sections of the response.

Evaluate Real Inquiry Responses

I made five inquires for vacation properties for a trip my family was considering. A lot can be learned by living the experience firsthand. Apply the characteristics of effective inquiry responses to these while thinking like a guest considering them.

I kept the inquiry text for the week simple:

Can you please give me the full rate information for this timeframe? Thanks

This did not tell owners anything about my interest level or vacation plans. The first response came in almost immediately.

Response 1

Hi Chris,

Thanks for your inquiry. Our condo is available for this time frame. The rates are as follows:

Rental fee	$	1,295.00
Damage Waiver	$	30.00
Management fee	$	35.00
Pet Fee		
Rental fee	$	1,360.00
Taxes	$	149.60
Total Rental Cost	$	1,509.60
Deposit		338.85

Please let me know if you have any more questions or if you would like to reserve our condo.

Glenda

The response is very concise. Glenda absolutely answered the question I asked and made it easy for me to see the total cost by highlighting. Unfortunately, the response is not visually appealing or compelling, as it is a spreadsheet pasted into an email. Glenda thanked me for my inquiry, but didn't go out of her way to make me feel welcome as her guest. The number of fees listed in the rate table makes me question how friendly and flexible she might be to work with. I sent out five inquiries; which condo was this?

Overall, this response looks like it was not much effort, and isn't very compelling.

Response 2

Hello Chris,

I have a two bedroom plus den oceanfront condo unit at the complex on the island. It has a 26' screened-in porch overlooking the ocean.

I do have the week of July 12-19th available at this time, at the rate of $1495 plus tax, Saturday to Saturday.

Regards,
Margaret

This response also answers my question but not completely. I am not sure what the tax rate is for this area and have to go back to the listing to look it up to do the math myself. The all-text-based response is not visually appealing. A 26' screened-in-porch overlooking the ocean sounds awesome. Actually seeing a picture of that porch while reading the response would be much more interesting. Then, I could visualize myself sitting there with a beer overlooking the surf. The dollar amounts being higher than the first response I got might matter less if I was reminded how great the place is. The response is concise but not particularly informative or friendly. This brief response leaves me with almost as many questions as when I sent the inquiry.

Response 3

Hi Chris,

It was nice to hear from you. Thank you for your interest in my condo. My property is available from Jul 26, 2014 to Aug 2, 2014 and I hope the dates work for you.

Our condo was totally gutted and renovated last year. I think you will like the expansive view of the bay and the location just across the bridge. I designed the kitchen to be easy to prepare meals at home so I have a lot of extras that you don't usually see in rentals. This is our second home so we planned the renovation for our needs and not just for rental.

The weekly rate for July is $865 which includes all fees and cleaning. The only additional cost is the 11% tax. Travel insurance is available but optional. For your convenience, we have a company that handles all the details while you are there. We believe a local contact is important for our guests. The deposit to hold your dates is $300. The remainder is due 30 days before arrival.

The island is a special place. I love chatting about it so contact me if I can be of help. I look forward to hearing from you and would appreciate a reply to let me know your thoughts and to confirm that you received this email. Thanks again for your interest.

All the best,
Cindy

dy's response isn't visually appealing, but is compelling as you read through the paragraphs. It sounds like a newly renovated place with a great view with lots of extras. The response requires quite a bit of reading to put it all together. There is a big risk that a guest with limited inquiry time wouldn't take the time to read it all. While the math isn't difficult, I have to do math to arrive at the total cost. Cindy seems welcoming and friendly and goes out of her way to make sure I feel comfortable asking questions. The price is quite low and this feels like it could be a contender.

Response 4

Good Evening Chris,

We are sorry it took a few hours to write back to you...today we loaded up our car with fresh new condo amenities and are driving there (from St Louis). We'll be there the week of December 7th. Thank you for finding us on VRBO! We would love to have your family as our guests.

We are available the week of July 26th.
If you would like to see more photos (VRBO limits the # of photos) of our condo please click (or cut and paste) on: http://www.abcd.com

The total rate (no other surprise fees/taxes, etc.) for the week would be:

Rent: $1395
Booking Fee: $35
Security Damage Waiver: $32.50 (Great Coverage but we can

make it optional, see note below.)

Tax (11%): $160.88

Total: $1,623.38

Deposit: $339

VRBO Discount: $35 off $1395

It is important to us that you receive excellent customer service, thus we use the assistance of a local rental property management company called Rentalz Co. because they can be like a concierge to help you with any needs you may have during your stay. They are located only a few blocks away from our condo. They are very helpful before and during your vacation. You can call them 24 hours a day and they will provide assistance if you are locked-out, maintenance issues, send/pick-up faxes, print boarding passes, etc. Annually since 2004 they have been winning awards for their excellent customer service and hospitality.

They also provide excellent housekeeping and cleaning services. We (and our guests) have been very satisfied with their cleaning responsibilities.

If you think you want to be our guests, we can access our owner's section of Rentalz Co. web site and block out your dates for 24 hours with no commitment and no deposit. We will also put a note in their reservation system to **subtract $35 from your rent amount** to show our appreciation for finding us on VRBO.

This will give you some time to check on airline rates and compare other condos. There is absolutely no pressure...if you decide to do something else the week would just be released back

101

into their availability system 24 hours later. Planning a vacation should be fun and stress-free.

If you do decide to be our guest and confirm your reservation...you only need to call Rentalz Co. at: 1-800-555-1212 (Mon.-Sat. 8:30am-5pm EST) and give them a deposit (you can use a credit card for the deposit). That will confirm your reservation.

There are some cancellation fees* if you cancel your reservation after you give Rentalz Co. a deposit. That is why we like to give our guests extra time to decide.

The following web site (you may have to cut and paste it) is also helpful because it explains the security damage/deposit waiver, deposits, procedures, final payment, electronic check option, optional trip insurance ($113.64), cancellation policy, etc.

http://www.rentalzco.com

If after reading the security damage/deposit waiver information you decide you do not want it (because you would be willing to pay for any accidental damage), you can let Rentalz Co. know (when making the initial deposit) that you don't want it. Only our VRBO guests are allowed to have this (security deposit damage waiver) be optional.

Rentalz Co. confidentially handles all the payments, paperwork, etc. You don't have to give a stranger (us) any credit card or personal bank check information.

They will process your deposit on your Visa or Master Card. The balance is due 30 days prior to your vacation and payable by personal or electronic check directly to Rentalzco. If you use a credit card for your final payment there is an additional charge of 3% to use a credit card for the balance.

We know this is a lot of information all at once... but it is better to have too much information than too little! Please feel free to contact us with any additional questions (about our condo, golf, bike rentals, restaurants, etc.).

Warm Regards,
Shirley

Shirley is very friendly in her response, but this email is overwhelmingly long. The pricing for the week was clear, however everything else in the email got confusing the more I read. What is the next step I need to take if I was interested? The response is not particularly compelling with the exception of knowing this owner likely takes extremely good care of their place. There seem to be a fair number of rules here, and it makes me wonder how flexible this owner would be.

It's easy to see clear opportunities to stand out. None of the responses used photos or branding of the vacation property. They range from extremely short to very long, but none seem to capture the guest's attention by taking them on vacation and telling them just what they need to know and no more. The responses didn't generally point out the key features of the property and took a fair amount of effort to read. Also, very few owners mentioned how much they would like to have the guest come stay at their property.

Creating the Standout Inquiry Response

With these standout opportunities in mind, you can create an inquiry response that will really capture your guests and get them booked at your property. This response will take your guest on vacation and help you connect with them. Like everything with your vacation property, this too should be easy and convenient. While the included inquiry response isn't terribly long, it gets a lot done.

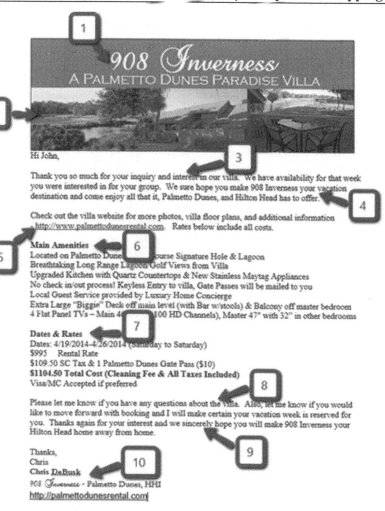

1. Use Your Vacation Home Brand

    The top banner of the email uses the same brock script font as the logo on my website. The background color is also similar. Keeping the logo and design consistent across all communications looks professional and may help your guest remember the property. The subtitle labels the site "paradise" suggesting of course that the property and experience will be heavenly.

2. Showcase The Experience With Pictures
The banner allows three pictures to be showcased. Choose these pictures carefully, as they need to be so good they draw the guest into the setting. The picture of the view from the villa and the front are both aimed to pull the guest into being there. The hope is that guest finds themselves sitting there thinking about driving up or looking out the window. The inviting bar table on the back deck makes you want to sit down and sip a drink with family or friends. All of these photos are early in the listing and web photo gallery, so the hope is also the guest will open the email and think, "Oh, I remember this place." Lastly, the banner with brand and photos provides standout visual appeal that hopefully gets the guest to keep reading.

3. Appreciate Your Guest
The text response starts friendly and thanks the guest for their interest. This is designed to project your genuine appreciation for the inquiry and opportunity to email with them about coming to your vacation home.

4. Connect With Guest
The response lets the guest know that you would really like them to vacation at your home. Guests will often send questions your way in their inquiry and the first

paragraph is a great place to address them. While this inquiry response doesn't have questions, I will start out with "First, let me address your questions….." This reinforces that you are listening and find their questions important. This paragraph is also a good spot to celebrate with your guests if they are excited about this family vacation. Let them know how great it sounds and you may even quickly highlight a family memory of your own from the place. Sharing in their happiness and sharing a memory is sure to foster a great connection between you and your guest.

5. Intrigue Guest with Your Website
   Entice the guest to your great property website to get them more engaged and involved in imagining their vacation. The sentence highlights additional information and details that will hopefully draw them in further, convincing them your place is the only one for them.

6. Highlight Key Amenities
   This easy to read bulleted list helps keep the reasons your place is great in front of your guests. Get your Marketing Plan out and make the list using the great features of your property. Some guests will bypass this section to get a look at the dollars first and that's ok. Hopefully, they will like the cost and go back to read the rest.

7. Outline Simple Dates & Rates
   Keep the costs really simple and easy to understand for your guest. This section calls out a couple line items

and clearly communicates the total cost. While fees are generally accepted in the vacation rental business, make your pricing refreshingly clear and avoid extra fees whenever possible. Adjust your rate, as additional costs need to be covered. Rate, tax and total cost is about as clear as it gets. Should you decide to discount the rate, include the listed rate, and then on another line tell them the discounted rate. Using their name is also a nice touch such as "Smith Discounted Rental Rate."

8. Encourage Guest Questions
    Make your guest comfortable to ask whatever and as many questions as they have. One guest and I exchanged a whopping twenty-four emails as she thought of more and more questions about the property. I encouraged this and answered them thoroughly and she ultimately booked. It was fun emailing with her and this allowed us to really connect while making sure she had the information needed for her important decision.

9. Welcome the Guest To Vacation
    The template welcomes the guest to make the property their Home away from home. The language reinforces that your property is a home and not some "rental place." It also invites the guest to make it their own. They can create their own memories and think of it as "their place."

10. Add a Professional Looking Signature
    The template closes with a professional looking signature. The lettering uses the brand look and includes the website URL.

The Goldmine Toolkit comes with the Inquiry Response Email Template as well as the Email Header to create this new inquiry response for your property. Go through each section of the response and modify it for your property. Feel free to use the general language verbatim. Your email client needs to be able to handle html email, but you should be able to paste the completed template into most email software.

What Is Your Guest Telling You in the Inquiry?

Now that you have a standout inquiry response template, you are ready for the next inquiry. Very few inquiries are the same and the first step is to read each word of the inquiry and think carefully about what your guest is telling you about them and their needs. Reading cues from the inquiry can be invaluable to effective response that ultimately results in a booking. Look at these actual inquiries as examples to see what can be learned.

Inquiry 1

Hello Chris - Although it will only be my husband and I making this visit, we're still interested in renting your place, which is WAY more than we'll need ... but it appears to be one of the nicest area rentals on VRBO. Please let me know how you wish to proceed. Thank you!

What The Guest is Telling You – This guest is ready to book, but without saying so directly would like a discount. While they may book anyway, a small discount would be a great way to start things off exceptionally for them and make sure you land this booking. I discounted the rate a bit for this guest and they were thrilled. Getting this booking for the week during off-season was excellent and certainly worthy of the discount.

Inquiry 2

Hi Chris. I live in your area & have all adult children. I am interested in renting your beautiful home for a family reunion with my two boys & daughter & one grandbaby age 6 months currently. I was not sure by your listing if one can actually swim at this area? Or does one need to go to a community beach? Is this area in a peaceful quiet location? Thank you so much for your attention.

What The Guest is Telling You – This guest is telling you a lot. This guest is connecting, which is a great place to start the conversation. She is pointing out that we both live in the same area which I suspect she learned by reading the Owners page on the website. This tells me she has invested quite a bit of time exploring the property as an option. There are quite a few questions, which also suggest she is a researcher. This guest seems almost ready to book. Connect personally with their family reunion and provide careful and detailed responses to the questions. Encourage further questions in the response so they can get comfortable with the reservation that it seems they really want to make.

Inquiry 3

We are interested in Jan/February 2015.

What the Guest is Telling You – This guest isn't saying much, but don't read too much into their brevity. It could be that they sent this inquiry to many owners, but it's also could be they have decided they want to book your vacation home. It probably won't surprise you that this inquiry was from a man. Men have a tendency to be brief. Don't tailor a thing in your inquiry response, as you just don't have enough information.

Inquiry 4

Please reply with confirmation of the availability of the dates and total cost.

What the Guest is Telling You – This guest may have sent this generic inquiry to many owners. Get to the point on availability and cost quickly to insure your guest can easily get the information they are requesting. They may not spend much time reading.

Thinking through what your inquiring guest is telling you can really help you craft an effective response. Also, spend a moment Google searching your guest to see what you can learn about them. Google searches are especially effective when the guest has a unique name. Common names often bring so many results that make it difficult to identify which of the Ann Smith's is the one who wants to stay at your vacation home.

Assuming you find your guest online, there are typically many interesting things you can learn about them. This information can be useful to get comfortable with them renting your place as well as ways you can best tailor your inquiry response. If possible, I like to get a sense of their age, interests, and professional background. Most guests are on Facebook and LinkedIn, which answers many of those questions. You can see a picture of your guest to get a sense of age. LinkedIn profiles provide education and vocation information. Beyond these sites, you occasionally find Pinterest boards, which can be enlightening to the guest's hobbies and interests. Thinking about the inquiry response, you can change the order of the main amenities list to bring forward different key features based on what you learn. I had a guest recently who I learned was a home stager. In the inquiry response, the top of the list consisted of updates to the property and stainless appliances. I figured this guest would have a keen eye toward high-end interior finishes based on their vocation.

Spend a couple minutes reading the inquiry carefully and researching your guest online. Research can pay big dividend in getting you comfortable with them in your home and help you bring forward the features most likely to turn the inquiry into a booking.

The Silence Can Be Deafening

You did it all right! The standout inquiry response was tailored to your guest and you really felt like you connected, but they didn't respond. If you have been renting by owner for a while, you know this situation all too well. It's ok. Guests sometimes take a while to come around, they might come back to you a year later, or you may never hear from them again. I typically don't do much follow up on inquiries. Folks will find you if they are interested. Occasionally, I will send a single follow up email to make sure they received the response and ask if they have any questions.

Connecting with Your Guests

"Get closer than ever to your customers. So close that you tell them what they need before they realize it themselves." – Steve Jobs

Since you are reading this book, you are no doubt committed to giving your guests the best vacation possible. For actively involved owners, a big part of this experience for guests is working with the owner. Connecting with your guest early gives them a glimpse of what it will be like to work with you. Strive to convey some key things to them from the very first interaction.

You are Interested in Them and Their Vacation – Thank your guest in the inquiry response for their interest in your vacation place. Guests will often share details of their planned vacation inquiries, about their cousins they haven't seen in ages or getting the grandkids together. Celebrate this with them by saying something in your response like, "Sounds like you have a great family vacation planned." The sentence doesn't overdo it, but shows them you care about their planned vacation, which is extremely important to them. Obviously, don't make it salesy like, "Our vacation home is the best in the area for family vacations." Connection with a guest is about them, not you or your place. Add a sentence or two about your guest and their vacation plan to the inquiry that shows you hear them and you care.

You are Responsive – Most listing sites prompt owners to respond to inquiries quickly to get more bookings. A swift, standout response can go a long way. Better yet, follow that with quick responses to all their questions. Help your guests in any way you can, including following up to find out things for them in response to their questions.

You Have Your Eyes on the Details – The single biggest way to do this is to make certain that you don't make mistakes in your inquiry responses. Simple mistakes can undermine guest's trust that you won't mess up their vacation with an error. Guests are giving money to someone they don't know, and hoping that everything will be all set when they arrive. Triple check your numbers and response text before hitting send.

You are Easy to Work With and Friendly - Friendly can be accomplished through word choice and tone. Add "Hi" to the beginning of the inquiry response to demonstrate a friendly salutation. Sounds simple, but good manners go a long way: include please and thank you. An informal tone can be quite effective to communicate to guests that you will be easy to work with. Guests often rent directly from the owner to escape the rental company rules, and sounding too formal can be interpreted as inflexible. Use words like "request" if you are flexible on certain points such as deposit amount. "We request a 50% deposit to secure the reservation." Where flexibility is possible, avoid absolutes like "required." One of the best ways to demonstrate flexibility is to work with guests in response to their questions. Find creative deposit schedules or give them booking options that get both guest and owner what they need.

Connecting with guests is largely being the friendly and responsive owner you would want to work with. Don't overdo it and run the risk of spooking or boring your guests with a long narrative about your last trip to the vacation home. Add a friendly sentence or two to your emails and tell your guests that you care about their vacation. Vacation is a big deal, and they will see how much you care once they book and come to your home!

When to Give a Discount

Conventional wisdom on discounting would say "never" or "only when asked." Both of these approaches are short sighted and don't capture the power of discounts. In a book about maximizing rental income, it may seem odd that I am advocating proactive discounts. Discounts should be used to make sure you get the particular bookings that you really want.

In vacation areas during peak seasons, discounts are not generally advisable. Fair pricing, great guest experiences and good marketing as outlined in this book will book your peak season without need for any discounting. One exception that you should consider in the peak season is for your returning guests. I give all of my returners the prior season's rate, which insures they always pay less than the published rate. This typically isn't a great deal of money, but is an important token of appreciation for their continued business. Returners are the best guests, because they clearly value the great guest experience and you know from experience they will take great care of your home.

The shoulder or off-seasons are the best time to give discounts. Since the volume of prospective guests during these timeframes goes way down, you need to work harder to get the bookings you really want. Presumably, your guests checked the pricing before sending you an inquiry, so you know they would consider the pricing in their budget range. Guests who want to spend time looking around likely have many options during these times of year. The absolute best time to discount is when booking the timeframe is unlikely otherwise. With one of my properties, weekend rentals are typical in the off-season. If an inquiry comes in from a guest requesting four nights, it is a prime discount candidate. Money for four nights is much better than two, even after a discount. Make darn sure you get that booking with a rate offer that the guest just can't refuse. You both win!

Desirable guest demographics is also worthy of discount consideration. A couple renting your home is likely to mean less wear and tear than a large family. Retired couples are particularly appealing, as they may leave the place better than when they arrived and likely have time to come back regularly. Guests who request discounts tend to not be good candidates for them. Often, these folks are looking for deep discounts that I don't recommend giving. Their strong priced sensitivity isn't a good match for what needs to be paid for great guest experience.

Lastly, how much discount? Round numbers like $50 or $100 off tend to be impactful to guests. Ten to fifteen percent is the range to consider when your property is priced competitively. A bigger discount than that would take unnecessary precious money from your pocket. They may have been ready to move ahead at the full rate, so keeping it modest says you appreciate them without breaking the bank.

Reservation Requests – Getting it all Right
The perfect situation is where no inquiry response is needed at all – The Online Booking or Reservation Request. This is when the first thing you hear from the guest is that they are ready to book and have done deposit and rental agreement approval. The

booking required zero additional time or effort from you and you can just click accept and thank the guest for their reservation. If you get a lot of these, clearly you have everything right for the guest to feel confident without needing to correspond. The reservation request can save a lot of email time.

When It Doesn't Work Out

Sometimes it just doesn't work out. After communications with your guest, something didn't come together for a booking. Perhaps the time they wanted was booked while they were making their decision, or they had too many people in their party for your place. Whatever the situation when it doesn't work, helping the guest find another place is a great step that can build strong relationships not only with this guest but also with other owners where you may be sending referrals. What a memorable experience to have an owner help you find a great place for your vacation. That guest may go back to the same vacation rental, or may remember you and how much they liked your place when they are looking around next year. Either way, the goodwill generated could pay big dividends down the line. And to think, all it took was a couple emails.

Gold Mining Tips
1. **Respond extremely quickly to guest inquiries.**
2. **Make your inquiry responses compelling with pictures, flexible tone, and welcoming text.**
3. **Connect with your guest by using information provided in their inquiry to celebrate their vacation.**
4. **Encourage guest questions and provide just enough information to make a decision.**

5. Provide a discount to guests when it's advantageous for you such as hard to rent timeframes.

6. Strive for as many online bookings as possible as they are efficient for everyone and show your listing is compelling.

7. When it doesn't work out for a reservation, help guests find another place as the goodwill to other owners and future guest visits can really pay off.

Chapter 8 – Booking – Make the Reservation Easy!

"Make your product easier to buy than your competition, or you will find your customers buying from them, not you."

– Mark Cuban

Vacation rental reservations are often not easy. Sometimes, they require speaking to someone on the phone and giving them lots of information. Fortunately, most everyone is accepting credit cards now, a big convenience to guests. But, guests may be required to sign and send back a rental agreement and a security deposit check. Seems like a lot to do. As a customer of anything, it feels odd to jump through many hoops to give someone money. It has to make you think these processes were created for the convenience of rental companies and owners.

With internet technology, reservation tools are available that can make a reservation a matter of a few clicks. This is how it should be. A guest reservation may be work for you, but should be simple for your guest.

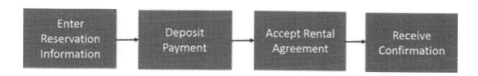

This entire process should be done online without any phone calls, physically mailing checks, or rental agreements. Draw a few boxes to demonstrate what your current reservation experience is

119

for guests. Keep in mind that this is the guest perspective and not yours. If each step is done online, it should take no more than ten minutes.

There are two basic paths of reservation. The first is a reservation the owner sets up following some inquiry email exchanges. Using the inquiry response from the previous chapter, you will need to send a bit more information to the guest to make sure they are good with the deposit and payment schedule. The Reservation Email Template has a format you can use for this email. Add anything else that you think the guest should know before booking. The second path is an online reservation that the guest sets up that combines all of these steps into one.

Stay Away from Reservation Fees

Somehow, it has become an acceptable practice for some rental companies and resorts to charge a reservation processing fee. In theory, this fee is similar to a registration fee. This type of fee can be an irritant to guests and should be avoided. Charge your guests minimal fees to keep your pricing simple and avoid them needing to pay a fee to pay you rent. Fees to pay in order to pay someone money aren't sensible. If you need to get additional rental revenues to cover costs, just adjust your rate accordingly, versus piling on a fee to pay more money. Reservation fees seem frivolous and don't set the stage for a great guest experience.

Crafting the Right Rental Agreement

There are lots of good example rental agreements on the internet; however, the Goldmine Toolkit contains one you can use for one-click approvals. It's important that the rental agreement and rules work for you and your property. With so many good examples out there, there is no reason to start from scratch. You may desire to stick with what you have or modify the agreement in the toolkit. Whichever approach you choose, a brief rental agreement that focuses on the most important aspects is best.

The purpose of the agreement is for your guest to clearly understand what they are signing up for, and get you the coverage you need. As an owner, you may be flexible on many things, but the rental agreement is the right place to make sure those non-negotiables are clear. No smoking or pets are the big ones for my properties and this is consistent with my listing, so hopefully this is no surprise to my guests. Most rental agreements sound very formal and not guest friendly, but you can make it painless by keeping it brief.

Important areas to outline in the rental agreement include:
Occupancy Rules – How many are allowed
Cancellation Terms and Policies – Under what conditions can guests cancel
Arrival & Departure Times
Homeowners Association or Area Rules – Rules on everything from parties to parking
Homeowners Are Not Responsible for Guest Harm or Actions

Keep it simple for your guests and you. One to two pages should be plenty to outline the important terms. Have an attorney read over the document if you make significant changes to make sure your interests are properly covered.

The Security Deposit Dilemma

Security deposits are a pain for guests and owners. While there is plenty of industry precedent for this generally accepted practice, security deposits can add complexity to the reservation process. The dilemma is whether it is ultimately worth the trouble.

Unfortunately, guests sometimes do things that create additional costs. It's natural to want to not be left holding the bag. Ultimately, the guest should only need to shell out cash if there was damage or extra cleaning needed. There are a number of options on how to accomplish this, but each of them has downsides.

1. Hold a Physical Check – This is the most yesteryear security deposit method, where the guest needs to mail a check to the owner or a property management company to hold in the event of damage or extra cleaning. Downsides to this option include the guest hassle of mailing this and the chance the check may bounce (which is likely minimal).

2. Credit Card Authorization – Authorization means that the charge doesn't actually occur, but a hold is placed on credit card funds in the event that it is needed. The positive of this option is that it technically doesn't cost the guest anything unless you process the actual charge. It does however affect the guest's ability to spend if they are close to their credit limit. More importantly, it's complicated to explain and execute. Ultimately, the guest may dispute the charge and leave the owner with nothing.

3. PayPal – This payment service is great for owners since the funds come into the account immediately, and can be refunded with a couple of mouse clicks post inspection walk through. The big downside to this method is that it requires your guest to shell out the cash for something that will usually be refunded back to them. Not particularly guest friendly.

4. Credit Card Charge – The guest could pay the deposit via credit card and then get it refunded back. Unfortunately, the owner would need to pay fees for money that is ultimately going to be refunded. The most expensive of the options by far!

5. Damage Insurance – This approach is very clean for the guest, but requires coverage purchase that very likely won't be needed. There are coverage limitations to these policies, as they only cover accidental damage. If a guest does purposeful damage, this insurance would not cover it.

Unfortunately, many of these create extra steps for guests or the need to part with money that will ultimately be refunded to them.

The Case to Eliminate the Security Deposit

"The owner made our booking and arrival arrangements so seamless for us."
– Voice of the Guest

We all have worries about issues with damage or theft in our homes. Examples could include TVs being broken or stolen, or damage to appliances. Security deposits typically aren't sizeable enough to cover these large ticket expenditures. A few hundred dollars just doesn't go very far. In many ways, we just have to come to terms with the fact that the risk of theft or big damage exists when we open our front door. Fortunately, these situations are extremely unlikely to occur. Most guests will treat your home with respect and leave it in the same condition as when they arrived, which is why almost every security deposit is fully refunded to the guest.

Security deposits are effective in large part because they keep guests on their best behavior. Vacations are expensive enough, so who wants extra costs? Instead of collecting a security deposit, the threat of charging for damage or extra cleaning can have the same effect and is must guest friendlier. Adopt the clause in the Goldmine Toolkit Sample Rental Agreement that reads as follows:

<u>Damage Deposit</u>: Guest understands that their credit card may be charged for up to $200 for damage or additional cleaning required beyond the standard checkout cleaning. Guest's credit card will not be charged a damage fee unless required post check out due to the above conditions. There is no prepayment of damage deposit needed.

By approving the rental agreement, the guest acknowledges they may be charged for damage or extra cleaning. The agreement language also calls out the guest friendly practice of not pre-paying a deposit. The possibility of these charges should make the guest careful to leave the property in good shape. Cosmetic issues such as carpet cleaning and simple repairs are a cost of doing business and generally not worth the effort to collect the deposit.

Practically speaking, this approach has downsides like the options above. If you use HomeAway Payments, the guest must approve and pay the charge. There is a lesser degree of certainty that you would get your funds in this model than if you were holding a check that could be cashed. The owner has every right to expect payment if the circumstances warrant, but the guest may decline the charge. That said, the careful behavior of guests is what we all want, and the mere threat of extra charges should be enough.

Security deposits are very much embedded in the vacation rental industry and I expect many owners will still want the additional certainty of cash in hand. For lower dollar amount deposits, the additional guest inconvenience and owner work often isn't offset by the nominal risk coverage. This is a plea to keep it simple for everyone.

Your Guest is Ready to Book, So What Next?

After your standout inquiry response and possibly a few courteously answered questions, your guest has decided your place is for them. They send you the following email:

After some homework, we have decided to rent from you for our vacation.

What are our next steps?

Anne

Now your work begins. Make sure your guest is good with the deposit schedule and is very clear on the next steps to get everything set for their reservation. Using the Reservation Email Template, respond with the following:

Anne,

That's fantastic news! We are so happy to have you as our guests. I will setup a reservation, which will secure the time for you. There are just a couple quick things to do and we can get that rolling.

Deposit & Payment Method - We offer credit card payments as a convenient option for you if that is your preference. If so, we use XYZ payments, which are provided by PDQ. I would send you a link and you just put in your card info. We request 50% to secure the reservation, and once we receive the first deposit, your reservation is confirmed!
Deposit 1 (Now 50%) - $XXX.XX
Deposit 2 (July 1 Remaining 50%) - $XXX.XX

Just let me know if you are good with this schedule and if you would prefer to use a credit card for payments.

Rental Agreement – The rental agreement can be approved online while you pay the deposit for credit card payments. Otherwise, I can send you the agreement directly via email.

So in summary, please let me know how you would like to pay and if you are good with the deposit schedule. Then, I will get the reservation going.

Thanks again, Anne - we are very excited to have you stay at the villa. Just let me know if you have any questions or concerns with the above.

The tone of the message is designed to be appreciative, friendly and informative.

1. **Immediately Welcome and Thank Your Guest.** The term "guests" has a welcoming ring to it. "Guests" is a term you might also use if you had some friends over.

2. **Tell Your Guest the Next Step and Do the Reservation for Them.** You could ask them to use a "Book It Now" type functionality if you have it setup, but they chose to talk to you first. So make sure the guest knows you will do the work to make things easy for them.

3. **Outline Payment Options & Let Them Choose.** Almost everyone will likely opt for credit card payments, but give your guest options. Regardless of what is ultimately picked, everyone likes options.

4. **Confirm the Payment Schedule is Good.** Ask permission to insure the guest is okay with the outlined payment schedule. When it comes to money, verify and put the guest in control.

5. **Highlight the Simplicity of Rental Agreement Approval.** If done online, this is just a few clicks. Even if you need to email it to them, reading the pdf and indicating approval is not difficult. Make sure they accept the agreement should issues arise down the line.

6. **Summarize What You Need.** Recap the guest's next steps just to make sure they got it.

7. **Close By Thanking Them Again and Encouraging Questions.** Close on a positive and make sure the guest feels comfortable asking any questions.

Add any additional items you need to care for at time of reservation. A friendly and easy to work with tone helps turn the booking request into a booking. Once you get the booking entered into HomeAway or wherever you are doing payments, make sure to enter it into the Goldmine Dashboard. This will assist you in tracking deposits/payments and other critical steps in the guest experience for each reservation. Additionally, it will add the rental income to the Financials Worksheet automatically.

Reservation Confirmation Email

Once you received the deposit payment, send the guest a quick note letting them know their reservation is confirmed. You can use the Reservation Confirmation Email Template.

Anne,

Thank you so much for your reservation. We are very excited you are coming to <insert your property name here>. Your reservation is fully confirmed on the calendar.

Your final payment is due 15 days prior to arrival and a request for that will be emailed to you. Two weeks prior to arrival you will receive a few page write-up about the property and area to assist you plan for and during your stay.

Please feel free to reach out to me at any time with questions. I can be reached via this email address or on my cell at XXX-XXX-XXXX.

This is a simple email with three purposes. First, let your guest know their reservation is all set on the calendar. It also includes what to expect next so they don't worry if time passes and they don't hear from you. Finally, it establishes the expectation of your full availability to them. "Email or call with any questions at any time." This demonstrates a big commitment to your guests, so make sure you answer swiftly when they email or call.

What Guests Do Before Vacation

Depending on how far out the guest booked the vacation, there could be significant time until your next communication with them. Use the Rentals tab of the Goldmine Dashboard to help you stay on track with timing of the next deposit and guest communication. When you have many bookings or multiple properties, it can be a real handful to keep track of everything unless you have good tools for the job. Most reservation tools keep track of payments, but don't track guest communications.

How active guests are before vacation varies, but there are three areas that tend to be consistent. Think through how you can help them with each of these.

Complete Final Payment – This is a simple transaction, so there isn't a lot to do. If you created multiple payments for guests, you may need to send reminders in advance. Your reservation system should do this for you, so just track that payments happen as they should. Extra emails on payments may send the unintended message to your guest that the money is all you care about and that you are "hounding" them. The Goldmine Dashboard tracks payment due dates and colorizes cells when the time is near. This insures you can follow up early with guests if needed.

Plan The Vacation – Guests vary a lot in terms of how much planning they do before they depart on vacation. For some, planning looks like putting their things in the back of the car and heading down the road to your vacation home. They may like to wing it when they get there. For others, they may spend hours planning exactly what to do each day. These planners tend to be the same folks we classified earlier as Researchers while making their vacation rental decision. They may be very interested in recommendations on restaurants and other attractions. Create your version of the Welcome to The Vacation Property Template and send it to these folks early. If they ask questions not in the write-up, research and promptly respond as appropriate. You may be able to think of other suggestions based on your experiences.

Pack For Vacation – It's disappointing to go on vacation only to realize you wish you had brought things that you didn't. Use the Welcome document to tell your guests about the amenities of your property, which allows them to bring things that may really add to the fun. Examples might include Blu-ray players, gaming systems, fishing rods, and tennis racquets. Help your guests figure out what to bring by making them aware of the amenities of your home and surrounding attractions.

Create a Helpful Welcome Document & Use a Hospitality App

"The owner made it a point to setup the Glad To Have You app, offering your rental and area information right at your fingertips." – Voice of the Guest

A well put together Welcome document can help your guests get prepared to get the most from their vacation before they arrive. Many of my guests have commented how helpful this has been to them before and during their vacation. I also leave a copy of this document at my properties. Recently, HomeAway purchased an app called Glad to Have You, which allows you to put all of this information at your guest's fingertips. Being able to link through to phone numbers and websites right on their phones is extremely convenient. The app will contain the same general information as your document, but giving guests the choice of either makes sure less technologically oriented folks aren't left behind. Here are some suggestions as you think through what to include:

Access Information – Keycode for Lock
Arrival/Departure Times
Special Instructions – Trash Pickup
Wireless ID & Password
Electronics Instructions – TV, Blu-Ray, Gaming System
Guest Amenities – Books & Games
Outdoor Activities – Golf, Tennis, Swimming, Grilling, Biking
Attractions
Restaurant Recommendations
Local Map
How to Contact You

Welcome to 908 Inverness! We are extremely pleased you have chosen to spend your vacation time at the villa and hope you will truly enjoy every moment. This sheet is designed to provide info for your stay in order to get full enjoyment of the villa's amenities and what Palmetto Dunes/Hilton Head have to offer. Please take this with you to the Island as it has very important information for your stay.

Keyless Entry - Your Door Keycode is **XXXX**
To Unlock – enter code and turn the lock knob to the right
To Lock – enter code and turn lock knob to the left

Wifi – Wireless internet is provided during your stay. Enter the following:
SSID – 908inverness
Password – 83ki34ls

Arrival & Departure
The villa will be ready for you at 3pm the day of arrival. The turn day is a busy one, but if you need to arrive a bit earlier we can work with the housekeepers to see if we can accommodate an earlier arrival. Please plan on departing by 10am. There are no extra steps for departure, just lock the door and drive off. Have a safe trip home!

TV Instructions
A Universal Remote is paired with each TV. Each remote is labeled with tape on the back that tells you which room it belongs in. In order to use the remote, press the button at the top with the device you want to control and then press the desired button to control that function. For example, increase the TV volume by pressing TV button at top of remote and then Volume + key. Unless you want to change devices, there is no need to press device button again.

1. *Downstairs TV* has over 100HD channels. **TV input must be on Component for cable** so press Input Key on Phillips remote and select Component from the menu if cable TV isn't working. Blu-ray is HDMI1. Wii is AV1 which can be accessed by pressing the Input button on the Phillips Remote. **If you have the TV input set on Component and still can't get a picture, pull the power cord from the back of the Time Warner cable box sitting on the table, let it sit for a couple minutes, and then plug it back in so it will reboot.**
2. *Bedroom TVs* also have Phillips Universal Remote. **TV input must be on HDMI1 for cable.** Like the Downstairs TV, you can select HDMI1 by pressing the Input button on the Phillips remote and then scroll to HDM1, then press OK. Blu-ray input is HDMI2. There is a Time Warner digital converter that must be on for the TV to display cable.

Homeaway's Hospitality App categories are predetermined, but you have a lot of freedom with what information to include for your guests.

Glad to Have You App, Accessed 6/20/2014

Regardless of whether you decide to use the app, create the guest document. There is a wide variety of what you might want to include on this document. Think of things you like to do or that would be fun for your guests. Vacations are about experiences, and this is a way you can bring some to life for your guests, especially those who may be coming to your area for the first time.

Notice the template header uses the same branding and look as the Inquiry Response. This is another moment where your guests can imagine themselves on vacation as they are planning or packing. The vacation anticipation builds!

The first page covers the "must haves" around access and logistics. I include TV and electronics in this category as well. These areas seem to be the source of most questions from guests. Leading with this information hopefully eliminates their confusion and is handy when they pick the document up off the coffee table. An easy look for the Wi-Fi passcode means not having to sift through the entire document.

Page two delves into the vacation experiences. Since this is a beach property, ocean access is important and the document also includes information about other outdoor activities. Share your experiences with guests to give them tips on how to get the most from their time doing these activities. Note in the completed template that I give tips on different combinations of golf holes that can be played at twilight depending on how much time there is before dark. It's very gratifying to get emails from guests who tell me how much they enjoyed particular sequences of holes or came up with a new one of their own.

The third page finishes off with Restaurants, a very popular section. We hope our guests will go through the whole document, but with this layout, it seems pretty certain they will look at the first and third pages for sure. Close with contact info for you and their local contact.

Like the other documents created through this book, have someone read and help you edit to make sure it's easy to understand. Revisit this document often and add sections when guests ask questions about similar topics. When you are at your vacation home, think through the experience as a guest, and ideas can often pop into your mind that would be great adds to the document. Manage the size of the document so information doesn't get lost in a sea of words. The bolded text at the front of each section helps the reader navigate it quickly, however too much information can be just as bad as not enough. At a certain point, anyone's eyes glaze over. The guest experience is a learning process of listening and making adjustments.

When you send the Welcome document to your guests, use the Your Vacation Is Almost Here Template email with the document attached. The email celebrates that the guest's vacation has almost arrived:

Anne,

I wanted to drop you a note as time for your 908 Inverness vacation is almost here! Please review the attached document as it has important information for your trip and for you to have while you are at the property. This information is setup with the hope that you will be able to get the most from the villa, Palmetto

Dunes, and Hilton Head during your stay. Please print this and take it with you so you have your code and TV instructions in particular.

Let me know if you have any questions or need anything prior to or during your stay. Please do not hesitate to contact me at any time should you need something - XXX-XXX-XXXX. We are excited to have you and hope you have a fantastic vacation!

The email is short and to the point. It shows excitement for the guests vacation and introduces the document so they know how best to use it. The final sentences are a reminder to reach out if they need anything and a wish for a fantastic vacation.

Communication, Communication, Communication

"Perhaps the very best thing was the owner's excellent communication throughout the experience – I didn't worry about a thing. Thanks for a wonderful vacation!" – Voice of the Guest

On this guest journey with Anne, we have already communicated with her many times via email. Each interaction was short and purposeful at different stages of the guest experience leading up to their vacation. The themes of excitement around vacation and owner availability are prominent in each, along with demonstrating caring that she has everything she needs to get the most from her vacation. These themes will carry through the rest of the guest experience as we move into guest arrival and vacation.

Gold Mining Tips

1. Make the reservation process easy by making it all electronic and removing as many steps as possible.

2. Avoid fees whenever you can, and instead build any extra charges into the rate.

3. Keep your rental agreement simple and focus on the must have items.

4. Consider eliminating the security deposit and instead establish the understanding in the rental agreement that the guest may be charged for extra cleaning or damage.

5. Give your guests choice on payment options and schedule.

6. Create a helpful welcome document containing information about your home and surrounding area. This information can also be used with a hospitality app.

7. Keep the lines of communication open with your guest leading up to their vacation and always tell them what's next.

Chapter 9 – Vacation - Put Your Guests First!

"Start with the customer and work backwards."

– Jeff Bezos

It's hard to believe the guest hasn't even gone on vacation yet! Now is the time. Up to this point, you have singlehandedly created the guest experience, but this is about to get more complicated. When the guest hits the road and heads to your vacation home, you are suddenly reliant on others to make the right things happen. This moment matters the most to your guests, and making this part of the experience great needs more focus and attention than many owners invest. As Bezos recommends, all owners would do well to start with their guests and work backwards. So often, guest experiences are defined by what owners or rental company's value, not the guest.

Much has been written about ditching your rental company and keeping 100% of the rental proceeds. My hope is that many reading this are looking to make that move to go it on your own; others may already be renting by owner. It is essential to have local guest support to create a great experience, and chances are that this won't be covered by just paying your housekeeper every week. The local support you need for great experiences is not just reactive but proactive to the needs of your guests.

Your local needs for a great vacation guest experience include:
1. Someone you trust who shares your vision for great guest experience
2. A great attention to the details

139

3. Near 24/7 availability
4. A single local point of contact for your guests and you
5. Can get to your home in just a few minutes
6. Willing to go the extra mile for your guest

This chapter will outline your strategy for finding local support, but I must prepare you for the reality that it involves money. However, it doesn't need to cost a lot or anything close to the standard rental company commissions. You will be searching rental and property management industry players who might not share your priorities or care about guests the way you do. It will take effort to find the right local guest experience. The payback to you will justify the cost with a multitude of returning guests who wouldn't consider going anywhere else, and rates you can continue to edge up each season, because it's worth every penny.

When Your Guests Arrive
"You Never Get a Second Chance to Make a First Impression" — Will Rogers

An effective way to plan a great guest experience is to envision what it should be step-by-step. Envision the arrival experience for your guests.

Guest Arrival Scenario 1

It's been a long day driving from Michigan, and we have been in the car for thirteen hours. Finally, we drive through the resort gate and turn down the road to our vacation place. It's dark, but we can see the front light and interior lights have been left on to welcome us. The outside looks neat as we take the short walk up to the front porch. We put in the key code and turn the knob. As we open the door, we are welcomed with a clean and fresh smell and a bright interior. The temperature inside feels great. We put down the light bags we brought in and begin looking around at our home for the next week. Each room is very clean and the towels are folded specially for us and laid on each bed. When we get to the kitchen, we notice some supplies, but our eyes are drawn to a bottle of wine with a special message for us. Wow, this place is great and the owners have thought of everything. This is going to be a great week!

When you travel to your vacation home, see if this is your arrival experience. Even planning the experience above, I have encountered issues. Keep working with your local partners to get it just like you think it should be.

Guest Arrival Scenario 2

It's been a long day driving from Michigan, and we have been in the car for thirteen hours. Now, we need to stop outside the resort for our gate pass. Finally, we drive through the gate and turn down the road to our vacation place. It's dark and we aren't exactly sure which place it is. Finally, we find it! As we step up on the front porch, we notice a pile of used towels sitting in the corner. We put in the key code and turn the knob, but it doesn't unlock. It's dark and we can't see the paper with the code well enough to double check. We head back out to the car and look at it under the dome light. We see that we entered it right, and call the listed number, only to get voicemail. We use both numbers we have, and now must wait. Finally, the owner calls us back and gets the code set up properly. As we open the door, we are welcomed by a hot room and a bit of musty smell. We put down the light bags we brought in and fumble around for the light switch. Next, we need to find the thermostat to get the air conditioning turned on to cool things down. As we head into the living room, we notice a vacuum cleaner sitting in the corner. The kitchen looks clean overall, but a load of dishes has been left in the dishwasher. Did anyone know we were coming?

The guest in Scenario 2 may still have a good vacation, but the first impression is terrible. No steps were taken to welcome them and they were reminded a few times of the previous guests while they were trying to begin their vacation. Scenario 1 tells the guest they are welcome and the owners care about their vacation getting off to a great start. No one would intend to have Scenario 2, but without the right local steps to make sure the arrival is great, this absolutely could happen. Despite efforts, these events have occurred in the past at my properties or those I have personally rented. Given our guests have so many options, the events above may be just enough for them to vacation elsewhere next time. While unlikely that all of the issues above would occur at once, just a couple of them can ruin that magical arrival moment.

The challenge is that despite your very best intentions, you are reliant on local folks to make almost every one of these arrival steps happen. Unless your local partner understands the experience you want to create, it won't happen. Leaving it to chance may play out just like Guest Arrival Scenario 2.

Great Guest Experience Creates Guest Loyalty

"We have rented lots of places in the past, and we could just tell the owner has taken time and interest to make things special and comfortable for his guests. We will definitely return to this property in the near future!" – Voice of the Guest

The Goldmine System maximizes your rental income by developing a sizeable base of loyal guests who keep coming back. Better yet, they come back for longer stays, or multiple times a year. This keeps your calendar busy with returners and new rentals at higher rates.

Loyal guests typically make an emotional connection with your home and you. Think about a brand or company you are loyal to, such that you wouldn't give your business to anyone else.

143

Chances are your loyalty is based on your reaction to experiences with that company that stand far above the competition. Consumers generally don't do a lot of research to form these connections, but are instead based largely on emotions. Said a different way, loyalty to a product or brand has a lot to do with your feelings about it and the value you feel that you get.

To plan your target local experience, it's helpful to first look at the vacation feelings you want to create for your guests. These feelings will make your property stand out to such an extent that they wouldn't consider vacationing anywhere else.

Feeling #1 - That the property is extremely clean.
"The home was so clean and comfortable and was great to host a fun game night with reunited family and friends" – *Voice of the Guest*

Your vacation home can be the most beautiful and exciting destination on earth, but if it isn't clean your guests will not be happy! If you asked women what was most important for a great vacation rental, I am certain many would have cleanliness way up on their list. Bathrooms and the kitchen are essential areas of focus. Vacation rentals get a lot of use; they need thorough cleanings at the weekly turnover, and deep cleanings at least once a year. Without the deep clean, your home will not truly be clean. Certain areas will not be touched by weekly cleans. Light bulbs, ceiling fan blades, and the inside of cabinets are prime examples that can give your place a dirty look.

Well executed weekly cleans are essential, but can be difficult to get consistently. Your housekeepers need to understand your expectations for each clean. Depending on the quality of the cleanings, they may also need lots of feedback from you along the way as reinforcement. To eliminate surprises upfront, outline expectations such as high quality sheets/towels and window cleaning for your doors to make sure your standard cleans include these items.

No matter how good your housekeeper is, everyone makes mistakes. The last thing you want is the guest to find issues when they arrive. The weekly turn day is a very busy time, and even small oversights can leave a bad impression. Housekeepers will be extra vigilant with their cleanings if they know their end product will be quality checked. Ideally, your cleaning company will do cleaning inspections of their housekeepers work, but makes sure someone other than your housekeeper walks the home to check all the details. Double inspections on cleaning may seem like a lot, but it's difficult to overemphasize the importance of cleanliness to the guest experience. Don't let the pile of towels out front ruin that first impression!

Lastly, there are annual items that need to be done to make sure the weekly cleanings will produce the best results. Many rental companies recommend or require an annual deep clean. I do my deep cleans in December, as my properties are peak season in the warm months. This is a must, but is often an expensive line item. One way or the other, get this clean done, even if you do it yourself. Here are some important items in the annual clean:

- Every nook and cranny should be cleaned, including the inside of drawers, cabinets, under beds, closets. Think of all the things that typically aren't cleaned. Pull everything off shelves to vacuum and empty drawers.
- Go through your supply of pillows, blankets, and linens to make sure things are clean and replace as needed.

- Wash the mattress pads and pillow covers (which I highly recommend so your pillows will last much longer). Like the mattress, don't skimp on the pillows. Buying the good ones and covers makes them last a long time.

- Pull mattresses and box springs off the beds and make sure they are clean. It's amazing the things you will find under the mattress. Give the box springs a good vacuum. Also vacuum the floor below the beds.

- Clean the tub/sink drains. Put on some gloves and take the time to clean out your tub/sink drains. If you can't stomach this task, hire someone to do it.

- Evaluate your pots/pans. I replace the pots and pans annually or sooner. Tfal makes a nice set of non-stick pans that won't break the bank.

- Glassware – check that you have sufficient supply or does any glassware need replacing. I always keep an extra box of glassware in the owner's closets to replenish as needed.

- Take all the dishware, silverware, glassware and kitchen utensils out of the drawers and wash them in a special cycle in the dishwasher. Also wash any trays that may contain silverware or utensils.

- Pressure wash outdoor furniture and decks/patios. Keeping these clean is important and replace anything that doesn't clean up well.

- Inspect and dust all furniture.

- Clean the insides and outsides of all appliances.

- Touch up paint as needed.

Carpet cleaning and window washing need to be done at least annually. Fortunately, these aren't big-ticket expenditures. Carpets get a heavy workout through the busy season. Carpet cleans obviously get rid of any stains and make the most out of the weekly vacuums from the weekly cleans. Buy a good vacuum if your cleaning crew uses yours. I have found you get what you pay for here and any vacuum worth having is going to cost $100 or more. Plan to replace the vacuum every year, and hopefully it won't be necessary. As for window cleaning, sun streaming in through clean windows speaks for itself. Many vacation rentals have nice views and they will be even more spectacular through perfectly clear glass.

Keeping your property well maintained is an important ingredient to cleanliness and the overall guest experience. Well-maintained properties have contents that work well and look good. If you go to your property often, you can play a vital role in insuring the working order of your vacation home. Whether you or a property manager, someone needs to attend to the critical maintenance tasks. On visits to my vacation properties, I use the following list to make sure I am on top of my maintenance items.

1. Check all sink shower drains
2. Touch up wall paint as needed
3. Have HVAC maintenance performed twice a year
4. Change HVAC filters
5. Check that all towel rods are secure
6. Run cycles of all appliances
7. Turn on and test all electronics including testing remote controls
8. Change batteries in door lock, remote controls and smoke detectors
9. Turn on all lights and fans – replace bulbs as needed
10. Check plumbing for leaks and insure toilets are not running

11. Insure supplies are available – light bulbs, batteries
12. Make sure lockbox key is still available as backup

Feeling #2 - Property is equipped with even more than is needed

"When we were taking a break from the outside activities the kids loved the games, puzzles and Wii that were provided." – *Voice of the Guest*

Little things often make big impressions on our guests, so spend time equipping your home with things they may like and that you will also enjoy.

The most important area to make sure is well stocked is the kitchen. Typically, your guests will spend significant time on vacation preparing meals. Having a good supply of clean pots and pans is essential. Also, kitchen utensils, from corkscrews to cheese graters, make happy hour and meal prep a success. Stock up on serving dishes in case your guests have a crowd to serve.

Provide extra bedding, such as additional blankets and pillows. Buy good ones and leave the extras in each of the bedroom closets. Go ahead and spring for the more expensive, soft fleece blankets – your guests will love them.

Leave books and games in your vacation home for evenings or rainy days. This shows your guests you care that they have a good time when the elements don't cooperate. If you don't have extras around your house, yard sales are typically a great source of low cost games and books. Your local library may have some good used book sales as well.

148

Feeling #3 – I can get the most out of my vacation.

"The information package that we received prior to our stay was invaluable because it helped us formulate ideas as to what we wanted to do on vacation." – Voice of the Guest

Use the few pages of write-up containing information about the key amenities of the villa, local attractions and recommended restaurants. This will demonstrate to guests that you want them to have a great vacation by sharing your local knowledge and making sure they understand how to use things at your property. Additionally, it saves everyone time by eliminating many of their questions.

Stand ready as a resource for your guests on the area as they have questions. I bet all of us have answered countless questions from "How close is the nearest grocery store" to "What's fun to do in the area with the kids." You should not only be ready for these types of questions but should actively offer your local knowledge to your guests. You have likely spent a lot of time in the area around your property so you have lots of local intelligence that will be useful. Encourage your guest's questions by answering them fully and repeatedly asking for them.

Feeling #4 – There is always someone to help if I need something.

"The owner went far above and beyond to make sure everything was what we had hoped for. We will certainly be returning in the future!" – Voice of the Guest

I am sure you have heard stories like the one told in this vacation property review:

"**Ok, but rental company was unresponsive** - the check in process was a NIGHTMARE. They would not release any keys until 3:00 and the line of guests was around the building. It was sad how little the rental company cared about that. The cottage had a great view and huge living space. It would really be perfect with just a little TLC and a rental company who cared."

The local folks helping you create the guest experience can truly make or break it for you. Guests need a single local place to call to get help if something isn't working. There realities of distance mean you are away from your property you need help from someone you can count on to make the experience what you desire to create for your guests.

Later in this chapter, the topic of getting the right local guest support will be covered in detail. Give your guests a single point of local contact regardless of the hour of the day. This isn't an office number but a cell phone to call that will always be answered. Your cell phone can serve as the backup. This should be the primary person responsible for your local guest experience and your point of contact as well.

Feeling #5 - The Owner/Property Manager Really Cares About My Vacation

"The owner is absolutely the BEST to work with...constant communication line with emails, he really strives to make it an enjoyable vacation." – Voice of the Guest

As important as this is, it can be tough to do. The difficulty is the folks needed to operate a vacation rental work in an industry that doesn't excel in guest experience.

Some tips to make this happen:

1. Tell your prospective and actual guests that you care. Do this in inquiry responses, email responses to their questions, phone calls, and any other chance you get. Tell them you would love them to come to your home, that it's never a bother when they ask questions. Obviously, you don't want to overdo this to a point where it doesn't seem genuine.

2. Make yourself always available to your guests. You may not be thrilled to do this, but ideally, you are just a phone call away no matter the hour. Always make sure they have someone to call after hours if it isn't you. Give guests your cell number and answer it when folks call. There is

no better way to show them you care than by making them a priority.

3. Respond quickly! Whether closing the booking or helping a guest with the TV, respond promptly every time.

4. Limit the Number of People Your Guest Needs to Work With. The more people your guest needs to interact with, the more chances for the experience to go wrong. Always give your guests a single person other than you to contact. Insist your rental or property management assign someone to your property, and if they won't, then dump them! A single person should understand the experience you want to create and be committed to helping you create it.

5. Ask your guests for feedback. Tell your guests you always want to make their experience the best it can be so you would like to hear about what they liked and what could be better. Once they give you feedback (and most will), respond to it thoughtfully and strive to do what makes sense. Chances are, many of your guests would like the same things.

Feeling #6 – I am getting a great value for the vacation dollar

"WOW, the owner thought of everything! We were totally impressed as we rented other rent by owner properties in the past, but were never offered this extensive service." – Voice of the Guest

This starts with fair pricing. We covered pricing early on in the book, but research similar homes in your area to make sure you pricing is in line with the accommodations you are offering. When you can, offer your guests a discount off the listed rate. Even small discounts can often make guests feel like they are getting a good deal.

If you provide extra services such as onsite property management/concierge, make sure your guests know about them, as convenience and service create guest value. Services such as shuttles to the beach as an example can be a big deal to guests. Also, discounts on items like golf, boat rentals, and restaurants are also especially nice if not publicly available.

What are Your Guests Experiencing?

"It's the little details that are vital. Little things make big things happen."
— John Wooden

Most often, our vantage as owners to the guest experience is through the eyes of the guests who take the time to tell us what was good and not good. Instead of waiting for things to happen and hoping for the best, thoughtfully plan out experiences for your guests by thinking through situations before your guests experience them.

The best way to do this is to drawing them out in simple flowcharts. This includes each step needed to do in order to accomplish something on their vacation. These high-level steps drawn out make it easy to see the improvement opportunities that can make a big difference to guests. Scenarios to draw out would include things like check in, resolving an issue, using amenities, check out. Keep the steps simple, but illustrative of what guests are doing and experiencing.

Let's start with arrival. This is the guest arrival process the previous owner used for our first property. From here, you can see how easy and high level it is to sketch this out.

At first glance, it doesn't seem as bad as there are just three main steps. Like many processes, it isn't so bad when everything goes right. That said, this process does have opportunity for improvement. Before getting into these improvements, think through the "rainy day" version of each step. Rainy day thinking is what happens when this step goes wrong.

The first step is to get a pass for your resort so the guest can get access. Most guests wouldn't find this type of step atypical for a vacation check in. So what could go wrong? The most typical scenario would be long lines to get the passes. Check-in day is busy at any resort, and late afternoon is particularly so. After being on the road for hours, the last thing guests want to do is wait in line. While this is a workable inconvenience, our guest experience avoids every potential inconvenience to the greatest extent feasible. Worse than long lines, what if the guest arrives very late and the resort office is closed? Will the gate folks let them in? Most resorts have figured out how to make check-in happen 24/7, but issues may occur with records of guest stays and this becomes all the more likely with an afterhours process. Could the resort and guest get in touch with you in the late hours should something need to be worked out?

The second step is a standard on location lockbox for the guest to retrieve the key as a convenience. The most typical rainy day scenario is human error. Frankly, lockboxes aren't difficult to operate at all once you have experience with them. The same could be said with TV remote controls, but these are also often a source of significant confusion with guests. In other words, seemingly simple things are often not simple to guests. They may put the code in and despite the careful instructions, expect to be able to pull the front off the box and miss the lever to pull down. For whatever the reason, the guest may not be able to operate the lockbox and thus not be able to get into the place. A quick phone call could remedy this situation, but what if you or whoever fields it misses that call while the guest is standing on the front porch. Minutes would seem like hours after all that driving, and the guest may start second-guessing their reservation. Worse yet, that guest is reliant on the previous guest to have properly secured the key in the lockbox at checkout. Most guests will not have an issue, but the first one that walks off with the key by accident could cause an issue for the next guest.

The last step is relatively foolproof. Once the key is available, it would be quite rare to see a lock malfunction or for a guest to get confused about turning the key in the lock to open the door. When we purchased our first property, there were multiple locks on the front door – a deadbolt and a lock on the handset. This was a recipe for confusion as the handset lock didn't work particularly well, and two keys were required. One key is one too many and two, well you get the idea. So sometimes, even a tried and true approach can have its issues. We resolved this by replacing the door altogether with a single key code lock.

"I have to say, though, that the thing I appreciated most was the keyless entry to the property." - Voice of the Guest

All of this rainy day thinking hopefully has you thinking about how to make things simpler and more convenient for guests. So here is what I did after my "rainy day thinking."

I eliminated steps that could be done by our property manager or me. The resort passes can be secured in advance and mailed to the guest. The guest and owner both know that the guest will have the gate pass before they leave their home. No extra stop, no waiting, and no potential for a closed resort office that could make for a most unpleasant check-in. The elimination of keys by adding a code lock also takes the lockbox challenges away. Giving each guest their own key code adds an additional level of convenience and security. There are no keys floating around and no need for you or your guest to worry about anyone coming back uninvited.

The Vera Zwave system by Mi Casa Verde is a very powerful and cost effective lock solution. Mi Casa Verde charges no monthly fees, and the service can be accessed via browser or mobile device. Both Schlage and Kwikset make Zwave locks that can be purchased for less than $200. The Vera also controls other Zwave devices. When paired with a Zwave thermostat, the Vera allows you to adjust the thermostat remotely, a big money saver.

At the time of writing, Honeywell offers a Zwave thermostat for around $150. You can also purchase a water and temperature sensor for about $60 that can be setup to text you if it senses moisture or the temperature goes above or below a certain level. Vera text/email alerting is included with each Zwave device, which means the system can be setup to let you know when certain things occur at your property. Examples include bad pin code entered on the door lock, a pin code is changed, temperature falls below a certain level, or moisture is detected. These great tools for managing your vacation property remotely can be purchased on Amazon.

The lock logs also tell you who is coming and going. If you play out the rainy day scenario on key code locks, they provide some nice backup options. First, if the guest has trouble, they can call you and almost every key code lock now has internet access, which allows you to let the guest in and troubleshoot any issues remotely. If that fails, local guest support has their own key codes, and could come over on a moment's notice to save guests in distress. Lastly, don't ditch the lockbox just yet! Traditional lockboxes are a fantastic backup to key code locks. I must admit that years in I have never needed to use this last ditch effort to get a guest in, but the day may come when the key code lock needs to be replaced and the old key method saves the day until the new lock arrives. Three layers of backup is a lot, and I have only ever needed the first layer to assist guests through their first unlocking of the door. Better that than stranded guests.

Not to rush guests off, but while looking at check-in it makes sense to look at checkout as well. Check out processes are typically simpler; however, they may include stacking towels, stripping sheets off beds, and in some cases even some cleaning. If physical keys are involved, they need to be locked in a lockbox or worse yet driven to a resort or rental office for drop-off. Strive to make the checkout process a departure process where the guest locks the door and leaves your home. That guest flow would only have one box. That's even easier than my departure process when I leave our properties!

Next, investigate something seemingly simple like how to control the TV. Through vacation home forums, etc., I have seen and participated in a great deal of dialogue on how to eliminate cable costs. Like all who participate in these discussions, we are tired of cable companies who provide little service to continually charge us big money for our cable service. Canceling cable to cut costs for your vacation rental is missing the point of guest experience, as it is an owner centric action. Not everyone cares deeply about TV and movies on vacation, but most vacationers like to be entertained. In the continual pursuit of great and exceptional guest experiences, please do not cancel your cable service just because you figure guests don't care or can use a Roku or other such streaming device. Cable is absolutely way too expensive, but on your way to maximizing your rental income, don't focus on cost. Instead, focus on return and the high cable bills will be a small price to pay for your returning guests and higher rental revenues.

Cable TV can be complicated to use when you are getting used to a new system. Additional options like Netflix make it even more so. Below I mapped out the steps my guest needs to watch TV.

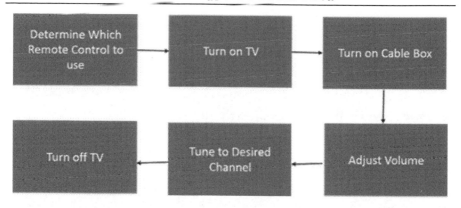

While there are many steps here, this doesn't honestly look too tough. Multiple remotes can be confusing, so a high quality universal remote that's easy to use can simplify this significantly. Better yet, a Logitech remote or other remote with macro capability can let you setup a "Turn On TV" button, which collapses all of this down to about three steps. There are many spots where guests can get confused. Which remote should I use? Why don't I see a picture after turning on the cable box? How do I find the right channel for the big game? The main point is by drawing out the steps and thinking of how to make it better creates an easy experience for your guests.

Included in the Goldmine Toolkit is a Guest Experience Worksheet that gives a framework to step through the guest experiences that make sense for your vacation home. Basically, it's empty boxes, but you can see from the example that this exercise isn't terribly difficult. Do as many situations as you can, from check-in/checkout to using the TV to convince yourself that you have made everything in your vacation home as easy for guests as possible. The quest to improve the guest experience is never over. Obsess about it. Think about the new remote control that makes it easier to watch TV. The new iPhone app that walks guests step by step through how to use things in your home or puts local restaurants and attractions at their fingertips. There really is no destination for guest experience, just the continual quest to improve and make things better for your guests by attending to all the details for them.

Once you diagram these situations out, think through the "rainy day" scenarios. What does the guest do when they can't figure it out or something doesn't work? You always need two or more "lifelines," as unfortunately humans are fallible. We could miss the phone call from our guest in distress. When you are on vacation, you don't want mistakes. Once you go through the rainy day experiences, draw an X through any step you can get rid of. Getting rid of steps for guests is a true victory, and they will thank you. They might just tell you how easy everything was, or they may specifically call out how they appreciated a particular thing you did for them to make things easy. We all want to hear as many of those as possible, as these "details" are often the very things that keep your guests coming back to your property. And, returning guests are the key to maximizing your vacation rental income!

What Happens When Things Go Wrong?

"Customers don't expect you to be perfect. They do expect you to fix things when they go wrong." – Donald Porter

No matter how much effort you put into the experience, it's inevitable things will go wrong. A guest will be stranded on the front porch, confused about how to get in, or the air conditioning will stop working.

One of my guests showed up for their Saturday check in to find the glass shower door in the kid's bathroom hanging dangerously off the track. I received a phone call directly from the guest and, as it was after 5pm, I called the rental company to get someone on call to go over to look into it. I wondered, why in the world did the housekeepers not report the situation? I asked these questions later, as we needed to get this fixed right away. I was pleased to learn the repairman could head over within the hour to get this issue resolved, and I let our guest know help was on the way. After a couple hours went by, I called the rental office to inquire on how this repair had gone. The employee I spoke with had no knowledge of the situation. A call to the repair contractor got no answer. With no information, I called the guest to ask them the disposition of the repair. This is clearly a situation no owner wants their guest to be in! The guest was very patient, but indicated the contractor had removed the shower door altogether and left. So now, we have an inoperable shower with no idea when this can be resolved. I placed numerous calls to the contractor to no avail. The absence of a shower door isn't the end of the world, but it did not get fixed until the following afternoon. The guests started their vacation with two days of significant inconvenience, and it sure didn't look like we had our act together when it came to getting this issue resolved. For hours, I had no information for the guest and little confidence that this was getting fixed quickly. I realized I needed a local point person.

It's impossible and unnecessary to try to think of everything that could go wrong, but it's useful to think of some main issue types:

Housekeeping Issue – While most unfortunate, these issues are typically straightforward to address. A call to your local contact or to the housekeeper themselves is typically all it takes to get this resolved. Guests often arrive late, so just make certain you have after hours housekeeping support.

Small Appliance or Electronics Failure (Coffee Pot or TV) – This is a more complicated issue, as you typically need someone to purchase a replacement and bring it to your property. I try to proactively replace coffee pots, toaster ovens before they go out. Then, you have a backup as you can store the old one in your owner's closet or attic. A local contact is ideal for this when you suddenly have something that needs replacing.

Damage Repair – Depending on the type of damage, you most likely need a contractor for this issue. If the repair needs to be done while the guest is there, coordination is needed unless you know the contractor's work, demeanor and quality standards very well. Depending on the type of damage, most repair situations are not emergencies but best cared for as swiftly as possible. The key is to balance the needs of the damage repair and inconvenience to your guests. If it can wait, it probably should. No one appreciates interruptions during their vacation, however if the damage is significant enough then moving the repair forward may be best.

Major Appliance or HVAC Repair – A major appliance failure is an urgent situation. Many HVAC contractors are accustomed to "distress" calls and can respond quickly. To get priority for the repair, it generally helps to have a maintenance contract with the heating and cooling company of your choosing. As a longstanding and regularly paying customer, you are likely to be well taken care of when your moment of emergency comes. Regardless of how much planning you do, it's a very unpleasant guest experience without climate control. Servicing your HVAC regularly is key to getting ahead of issues. Typical lifespans tend to be 12-14 years, so as you enter this range it can be a good idea to get your system replaced proactively, on your schedule. The system is going to quit sooner or later, so once you hit the high end of the range, begin looking to swap it out to take advantage of the lower energy consumption of a newer model.

As unpleasant as the HVAC situation above is, the major appliance issue may be worse. Typical appliance repair is not geared for quick service – especially if your appliance is still under warranty. For appliances like dishwashers and microwaves, you may be wise to consider a replacement. This is especially the case if your appliance has already given a number of years of service. Given the cost of ranges and refrigerators, dealing with repairs makes more economic sense. Make some phone calls to area appliance repair companies to make sure you have a couple at the ready. Most major brands are unimpressive when it comes to dispatching repair technicians timely, so you may need to just ditch them altogether to commission a local option yourself to get the repair done quickly. If your appliance is new, this could impact your warranty, so consider this a last resort. Do whatever it takes to get the job done for your guest swiftly as you can near the end of the warranty period.

Simple Question such as how to Use TV – Thank goodness guests most often have simpler situations. Even with instructions, it's completely understandable to have questions about how to use the TV or Blu-Ray. You may also be asked about other rainy day activities or many other topics. How to handle these can be a matter of preference. All things equal, the owner's touch on these is likely to be most effective and meaningful to guests. That's not to say local contacts aren't effective if they are good, but your guests will appreciate access to you. I give all guests my cell phone number, tell them to call anytime, and answer when they call.

There is no single right answer as to how best to provide guest support that makes their vacation special and gracefully handles the inevitable issues. The next chapter covers local support strategies with the hope of finding you the setup that is best for your guests and you.

Gold Mining Tips

1. **Work backwards from the guest to create great experiences**
2. **Live your guest's experience while visiting your vacation home**
3. **Diagram important guest activities and work hard to eliminate steps**
4. **Make guest arrival exceptional with a local team that attends to the details**
5. **Create guest loyalty by creating feelings that your property and service are superior**
6. **Thoughtfully plan the "rainy day" steps for your guests. Contingency is king.**
7. **Investigate Vera by Mi Casa Verde for keyless entry if needed**

8. Be ready for local issues by having a plan and repair folks on standby

9. Never stop working to make everything easier for guests

Chapter 10 – Creating Great Local Guest Experience

"BY FAR THE BEST VACATION I'VE EVER BEEN ON"

– Voice of the Guest

To have a great guest experience, you absolutely must have someone local you trust to make it all happen smoothly for your guests and for you. The local happenings for your vacation home will make or break your vacation guest experience. In addition to quality housckeeping and maintenance services, you really need someone you trust to manage all aspects of the local experience for you. Unfortunately, you aren't there to do it.

If you still need some convincing on local management, consider the following.

1. You Need Eyes and Ears You Can Trust – One of the toughest things about being a remote owner is being blind to what's going on at your property. From knowing your place is spotless clean for the next guest to making sure a simple repair is performed properly, a set of local eyes is invaluable. Once your local manager knows the experience you want to create, they can make sure it happens every day. Great guest experience is about quality execution and if you wait for the guest report to find out how things are going, it's too late.

2. When Things Go Wrong, You Need to Act Quickly – The moments things go wrong are the ones where you need your local manager most. When a guest calls because the refrigerator stopped working, someone should be at the property in minutes taking action. In moments of inconvenience during vacation, guests need to see that you are doing everything in your power to fix it fast. Most guests understand that things will go wrong from time to time, but slow response communicates that they and this issue are not important. Quick response to resolve an issue can turn a moment of challenge to a moment of delight; however, it's extremely difficult to coordinate local action and guest communication from a distance. Your local manager can be onsite making all of this happen while keeping your guest up to date on the

latest. Good local support can also triage issues that may also save you money. From making the repair themselves to negotiating with the contractor, a trusted local coordinator can often get it done right for the best price.

3. Guests Need Someone To Help – Vacation is a big deal to everyone who takes one and no one wants inconvenience. Flexible and responsive help to bring more towels or replace the coffee pot take effort off your guests while making sure all the details are attended to.

4. Peace of Mind – Given that you love your vacation home, my guess is that you worry about it. With vacation rentals comes risk that your property will be damaged or there will be theft. It's great peace of mind knowing there is someone you can trust keeping an eye on things. Frequent walkthroughs are not only a must for your guests, but also for your own peace of mind.

Ingredients for Great Local Experience

This chapter will cover the best way to create a great local guest experience and what it should be. In order to shop for differentiated local services, make sure you know what you are looking for, and that you can communicate it clearly to your prospective local team.

1. Thorough, Frequent, and Efficient Communication – Thorough communication tells guests exactly what they

need to know, and provides options for additional information. Frequent communication shows you care about things like how their arrival or vacation was. This is also communication with your guest throughout their time in your home. Efficient communication doesn't overwhelm with so much extraneous information that your message gets lost.

2. No Check In/Out Process – This is about making it super convenient for your guests. Instead of check-in and out, it becomes arrival and departure. Check-in would indicate something for the guest to do when they arrive. Aside from opening the door, everything else should be done in advance to make it easy.

3. An Exceptionally Clean Home for Every Guest – While logically guests know that other people stay at your vacation home, they shouldn't be reminded of that by anything left behind from previous guests. Cleanliness gives your guests that fresh start to make everyone feel right at home.

4. Get the Details Right Every Time – Marketing is great, but execution is what really matters when your guest arrives. The scary part is you almost completely rely on your local team to get it right, but when they are awesome, you can rest easy. Double and triple check things to make sure they are right. When the inevitable mistake happens, respond decisively and find a way to make it up to your guest.

5. Being Always Available to Guests – Rent by owner guests generally want and appreciate direct access to the owner. It stands to reason that the service will be better when you can connect directly with the property decision maker. Since you know your vacation home, chances are that you can solve their problems faster than your local partners who may have to figure out things you already know.

6. Going the Extra Mile – The extra mile generally means extra effort to meet guest needs. Fortunately, many things like early arrival or late departure times qualify. If a guest arrives to the vacation destination early, arrange it so they are contacted when the property is available for them. Listen to your guest's needs and make offers to them for things they might like. This shows that you value them and their vacation. If you know your guest is arriving late, arrange to have lights on for their arrival.

7. Provide Extras Free of Charge – Guest extras may be simple things like books or games. Movies are a great touch through a DVD library, or better yet access to Netflix so they can pick from hundreds of titles. Other ideas include bicycles or kayaks if you are near water.

8. Add a Special Touch – A welcome gift is a great way to show guest appreciation. Consider a bottle of wine or something locally appropriate. Welcome gifts can really stand out and get things off to a great start when your guests arrive.

What's the Best Way to Make it Happen?

Unfortunately, there is no single answer to this question. The best solution for each owner and property depends significantly on your guest experience priorities and what's available in your vacation location. Now that you have explored these needs in the previous chapter, this section will cover the main options to make it happen so you can make the best decision for you and your guests.

Before diving in to the options, spend a few moments assessing your current situation with local support. Answer the following questions:

1. Does your local support value and create great guest experience?
2. Do you have premium housekeeping services?
3. Can your housekeeping services be customized for your property?
4. Are you able to change things with their services for greater guest convenience?
5. Is there a single person assigned to your property for you and your guests?
6. Can you get in touch with someone local instantly to work anything needed?
7. Does your local support take on work for guests to make it easy?

The answers to these questions tell you how far you have to go from where you are currently. Arrangements such as Housekeeping Services, Rental Companies, and Property Management/Concierge Companies are all potential local support. Some have a greater likelihood of working than others do; however, the quality of the people and process is what really matters.

While you can find the right local support in each of the arrangements above, it's not easy. You are working to create a differentiated guest experience, and many of these services are geared to be average. Going out in the local marketplace to find something differentiated is a bit against the odds, but the steps outlined here will greatly increase your chances of finding that needle in the haystack.

Many rental and property management businesses offer full service of rental, property management and housekeeping. This makes it somewhat difficult to figure out what their main strengths are, and to evaluate whether they can really bring what you need. Conversations with the owners are critical to determine what the company's roots are. Where their business started is likely their strength. This information can give you clues about how well they may fit your needs.

Housekeeping Plus – Housekeeping by itself won't suffice, but some housekeepers have extended their services into property management offerings. I am covering this local arrangement first, as it is least likely to give you the full range of services needed for a great guest experience. Quality housekeeping is such an important part of the guest experience; it can be tempting to build local services from that strength. Great housekeeping takes excellent attention to detail, a fantastic trait for any local guest service.

Extending from housekeeping into a full range of local services can be problematic. Housekeeping companies tend to need volume to make money. More cleans mean more staff, more turnovers, and likely less attention to items such as maintenance. The breadth of local guest services can be more limited based on what is a logical extension for the owner or company. Also, housekeeping skills don't necessarily translate into guest experience skills. Great guest experience often requires guest interaction and coordination, which may be difficult for a service that is typically in the background.

Property Management – Property management companies have long provided services focused on the owner's needs to take care of the property from a distance. They typically are quite good at keeping an eye on things and coordinating necessary maintenance. Many have grown their businesses with additional services such as rental listings of their properties. To tap into the "rent by owner" market further, many of these companies are offering Concierge Services. This is a logical growth of their businesses if they do the full suite of rental, housekeeping and property management services.

Property management companies have significant owner interaction, which can translate well into effective guest interaction. A guest-focused mindset is more complicated with many masters to serve. The financial relationship with a property management or concierge businesses is typically straightforward. You pay a rate for services delivered, which can be quite effective and less costly than a rental commission based pay structure. High commission based pay must be avoided. The big question to answer with property management companies is whether they have what it takes to be guest focused and gracefully handle guest interactions. Talking to the property management staff and references is generally the best way to assess this.

Rental Company – Lastly, rental companies have also branched into concierge services, in large part to capture a slice of the ever-growing rent by owner marketplace. This seems a natural progression as the companies are already in the rental marketing and guest service business. Careful evaluation is needed to make sure the service delivered is good enough to differentiate your vacation home. Many rent by owner guests try to avoid rental companies due to the perceptions of greater cost or poor customer service. Unfortunately, there are some bad rental companies out there that give a bad name to the rest. Fair or unfair, it's an important factor to consider in your guest experience if you plan to use a rental company locally. Guests may feel bait and switched if they felt they were getting an owner experience, only to wind up with a rental company. There are certainly good rental companies out there; in particular, those with a concierge focus have a greater chance of success delivering a great guest experience.

The Rental Company Challenge

When considering rental company services, keep in mind some structural challenges that may impact their ability to be great at guest experience. They often get too big to pull it off. Before the internet enabled rent by owner options, rental companies were the only show in town. The rental business is more competitive than ever and the rise in rent by owner as a share of the market has undoubtedly put pressure on rental company revenues and profits.

All of this means that rental companies often need more properties to generate the margins they need to be profitable. Even if that isn't the case for specific rental companies, it's natural to want to grow to increase selection and the likelihood of greater profits. This growth in properties means they need to grow staff. More staff in their office calls for a standard guest experience. When you have lots of properties and staff, it becomes impractical to keep up with different experiences for each of them. Depending on the hour of the day, any of the staff members may be called upon to take action. Imagine if there were hundreds of properties, each with different rules for housekeeping, maintenance, and special touches for guests. It would be pretty much impossible to do this well, which is why many larger companies will not allow customization. Frankly, they are very smart not to. Not to mention, it's more difficult to deliver consistent and great guest experiences with more staff. Some folks will be great at it and others won't. If your property is just a number to the folks in the office, what your guests will get is a bit of the luck of the draw. Tough to like those odds.

With many vacation locales, it's not hard to book the peak season. Peak season is where the big money is made, and discounted rate commissions may not be worth the effort for the big companies. If rental companies can book the peak season being mediocre at guest experience, they may not have incentive to be great. A good way to assess this is to ask about is volume or percentage of returning guests each year. If many guests with lots of other options keep coming back to them, chances are they are doing it right. Also understanding the ranges of weeks rented annually is a good measure of how much they care about the non-peak season. Even if you aren't interested in marketing help from the rental company, this information is useful to assess their guest experience quality.

If you are currently with a rental company, or have been in the past, you may be familiar with the "why aren't they renting the place more?" scenario. Vacation rental companies are obviously in the business to make money. Your profitability isn't their primary concern. If a guest calls in and likes your property that's great, but if it's more lucrative for the rental company, they may be happier renting a different property. No one cares about your vacation rental revenues more than you do. High cost and low booking rates are key reasons that a rental company alone approach can leave a LOT of money on the table.

Please don't misunderstand the takeaway from this section of the book. I don't believe rental companies can't create great guest experiences. Quite the contrary, they are ideally positioned to do so; however, many of them don't because it's impractical to do on a large scale.

The Smaller Guys Can Do Better

Regardless which of the local partner types are the focus of your search, smaller companies can be more flexible. Being small doesn't automatically mean they are great with guests, but they can customize the experience and keep up with it. This is where your diligence comes in to determine whether they can, and are willing to deliver to your requirements. With a smaller number of properties to care for, these companies can have different "fingerprints" and execute well.

So how do you tell whether a small company can pull it off? First, you need to be talking to a decision maker. With the smaller companies, you should have access to the owner who can make the calls on guest services. Secondly, the smaller guys may be hungrier to get your business if they are looking to grow. They may sign up for more services to land your business. This will be especially true if they believe that your property will be lucrative. Also, the company owner may be more willing to sign up for additional services if you seem easy to work with.

Local Guest Experience is a Partnership

To determine whether you have the right guest support for a great guest experience, answer some key questions, such as, "Is my local support a partnership?" Do you feel like you are in business together to serve your guests? Does your local contact come up with new ideas to make things better? Do they share your desire to make your guest's stay great? Do they act immediately when there is an issue and make sure to always follow up?

If the answer is No to any of these questions, you should consider searching for a new partner. We will dig into the selection process in detail in the next section. As you talk to prospective local support companies, tell them upfront that you are looking to create a different level of guest service and that you view the relationship as a partnership. As you are renting by owner, you will be an active part of the guest experience, which requires a great deal of communication to make sure everything is smooth.

Once you are up and running with whomever you ultimately choose, hold up your end of the deal with solid communication and investment in the relationship. Communications include reservations, guest communications on issues, or other feedback. Investing in the relationship is getting to know the individuals who make things happen at your property. When you are at your vacation home, make it a point to visit your local contact, say thanks for all they do, and work on any improvements needed.

Finding the Right Local Partner

If you are just getting started with a vacation rental or decide you need to swap out your local guest service, do significant research to pick the right local partner. Make a list of around five prospective companies to consider. Internet searching works, but connecting with folks in your local market is likely the best source of intelligence.

Set up an appointment to discuss each company's local services. It's ideal to have these conversations in person, but it isn't always practical. Being in their offices can tell you a great deal about how they do things. Who is answering the phone or greeting guests that walk into the office? Are things organized? Are the employees friendly, and do they seem competent? Even if you need to interview these companies via phone, I strongly recommend an in person visit to the office of the company you ultimately choose. You will need to sign some sort of contract with them, and as we discuss later in the chapter you may need to do some negotiating. In-person negotiations are always preferable.

In the Goldmine Toolkit, you will find a worksheet to score each of the local service providers you are considering under the name Local Guest Service Selection Worksheet. This file contains each of the questions below with two fields to enter for each. The first field is a priority, which is denoted by a 1 for important and 2 for essential. Read each question on the sheet to decide whether the question could be a deal breaker and if so give it a 2. The other field is the score of 1, 2 or 3.

3 – Meets All Requirements

2 – Partially Meets Requirements

1 – Doesn't Meet Requirements

Capture notes so you can recall the rationale for particularly high or low scores. Add additional questions to the spots reserved on the sheet and score those, as well. No scoring matrix is perfect, but hopefully you will see the best companies move to the top of the scoring list.

Local Service Selection Questions

1. **May I speak to the owner about your services?** This is a great way to see how swiftly you can get owner access. If you can't get to the owner or a real decision maker, I would scratch the company from your list.

2. **How many properties do you currently care for?** To get the kind of guest attention you need, it's a strong likelihood the book of properties will need to be below fifty. This shouldn't be a deal breaker by itself, but above fifty properties give everything else a super critical look.

3. **Please describe what experience you strive to create for guests and how that differs from your competition.** This should be an easy question for a company who really knows what they are doing with guest

experience. If they struggle to answer, they may just be a "me too" option.

4. Tell the owner about the experience you want to create for your guests. You could provide them the Local Guest Experience ingredients in the first part of this chapter. Better yet, put it in your own words. **Do you currently create this kind of experience for any of your owners?**

5. **Since I want a great guest experience, how do you handle new services or changes I want to make for my guests (upgraded towels, complimentary bottle of wine, etc.)?** Gauge the flexibility of the response. Some companies may say no or yes for a cost. If you get a yes, inquire about the cost of a couple examples to make sure there are no surprises. If they say no, scratch them from the list. With no ability to tailor the experience, you will not be able to set it apart from your competition.

6. **Do you assign someone at your company specifically to individual properties you support? If you don't currently, are you willing to assign a point of contact to me?** Companies that naturally do this get the power of a single point of contact to get to know the properties and guests. If they decline to do this, strongly consider scratching them from the list. Multiple contacts make it very difficult to create a consistently great guest experience.

7. **How do guests get in touch with you? Do you have 24-hour contact options? How does this work?** Any rental/property management company worth its salt has a 24/7 contact method. The question is, does it really work? Also, how is it supposed to work? If a guests calls in the middle of the night because they can't get into the

property or has some kind of emergency, what happens then? Insist on knowing who monitors the 24/7 line and response time targets.

8. **Do you know how satisfied your customers are with your services?** Smaller companies generally don't measure this, but it's interesting to know how the company views owner and guest satisfaction. Measurement demonstrates they care.

9. **Can you please give me two references of existing owners I can speak to about their experiences with you?** While the company will surely pick owners who will have positive impressions, you will be asking the owner detailed questions that should provide great insights about strengths and weaknesses of their services.

10. **How do you make sure your places are clean for guests when they arrive?** Relying on an experienced staff of housekeepers isn't good enough to make absolutely certain the property is clean. The only way to make certain is to check and inspect. Multiple sets of eyes are always best, and an independent inspection of the cleaning is ideal.

11. **When things break, how do you get them fixed?** An experienced local service company should have this down to a science. Listen for a dedicated staff or the use of common contractors that can be trusted. Ask how they manage the repairs and what steps they take to make sure that guests and owners are properly informed of the latest status.

12. **How does your pricing work and how much would I expect to spend on a monthly basis?** It should only take a couple minutes at most for the owner to explain

how the pricing works. If it takes longer, it's probably just too complicated. Ask if they are open to a simpler pricing structure.

13. **Under what conditions (if any) do I need to pay you beyond your commission or standard rate?** This is a good vantage into the fine print of the rental agreement or any hidden charges. Make sure there are no extra fees to manage repairs or onsite activities. An hourly fee could really add up on top of the repair cost you are already paying.

Conduct Reference Calls With the Top Scorers

Ideally, the company will allow you to pick the properties for your reference call. They may not want to bother their other owners unless they have already said they were willing to conduct a reference call. If you get the opportunity, pick a property just like yours and then find the most upscale property they manage. Otherwise, ask them why they picked that particular property and owner. Hopefully, you hear about the longstanding relationship with the owner and similarity to your property.

There is no need to score the reference call, as it is really just designed to inform your scores with real life examples from one of their customers. There is significantly more power to hearing about responsiveness, suggestions and great guest experience directly from another owner. As you ask questions, just jot down notes and revisit your scoring sheet for revisions if needed.

Negotiating The Best Price

Now that you have found the right local partner, maximize your vacation rental income by not paying too much for their guest services. Many property management companies charge a flat rate for their services, but working with the owner hopefully facilitates the negotiation of a rate that works best for your budget. The term negotiation implies that you are interested to not pay the listed price for the services. This conversation is best done in person.

There are two basic pricing structures for local guest services: fee based or commission based structure. One is not necessarily better than the other, and you may encounter some pricing structures that are a blend of both. Simpler is usually better and blends can get complicated. As pricing gets complicated, it makes the cost unpredictable. This can create conflict between you and your local team. Frankly, no one wants that. After all, you are looking to work together for the common good of your guests, not to bicker about a $50 service charge. Chances are you will find more fee-based pricing from property management companies, and commission-based from rental companies.

While you were asking the above questions of all the local service contenders, you gathered some pricing intelligence from your local market. Hopefully, you saw some good examples of both types of pricing models and got a good idea of how much the services cost. If you didn't get good pricing information, just make a few more quick calls to see what else you can learn. If you selected the lowest price option, the pricing intelligence helped you get a good deal. You may have selected an option that wasn't the lowest price, and this is where your pricing research can really pay off. Figure out what your annual cost is likely to be, and use the lower price from the company you didn't select to negotiate.

Competitor Comparison Negotiation Strategy - If you are working with a company with a fee-based structure, you are looking to negotiate that rate down. This is just like haggling with your cable company by threatening to switch. You just got this great offer from Comcast. You really like them best, but you might have to switch cable companies for this great deal. Could you match it for me? So in this case it goes like:

"I have also been talking to Mountain Property Management and they seem to have some similar services and I really like their prices. I would rather go with you because <insert something that wouldn't raise the cost> you really seem to have good people. Can you match their price?"

Now, it's the owners turn to respond. You may hear they can do that price and mission accomplished! You may instead hear "They don't have the same quality housekeeping and charge more for service calls."

Good local service companies know their competition, and they may be right. After all, you didn't pick them as your first choice either. If they didn't come down at all, then I would say something like "I hear you, but that's the price I need to make the move." This tells the owner that you are serious about this price and they might make a counteroffer. "Well I can't do that, but I can get close…" The owner may also just hold their ground. If the owner makes no movement, then thank them for their time and hang up. Just like when you buy a car, you walked out of the showroom. Assuming you don't get a call back within 24 hours, you found a price that owner just won't do.

After a couple days have passed, call the owner back with a counteroffer. If that doesn't work, then see if you can get some services added in or consider whether any of the other local service options should be reconsidered. If all that excellent negotiation didn't get you anywhere, you may just have to pay what they are asking. They may be the best, and in the end, it's worth it.

Budget Based Negotiation Strategy – You may not have found good competitor pricing information or if you are negotiating with the company with the lowest price, you can always use a budget number. Generally, this tactic is less effective than using market pricing from a competitor but it may just work. Decide a dollar amount that is a reasonable reduction off the standard pricing. Reasonable might be a 20-25% reduction. Going higher than this is likely to be insulting and generally ineffective. Once you have your number, you are ready to roll.

"I really like the idea of working together, as you seem to have really good people and guest services. To stay in line with my budget, the maximum I can pay is X. Do you think that can work? I think we would work really well together."

The owner may say yes, give a counteroffer or flatly decline. The counteroffer may be ok if close to your number. A flat decline is a bit tougher to deal with but don't be discouraged just yet. Relate to the owner a bit to see if there is a way.

"I get what you are saying and totally understand that there are lots of expenses to cover. Is there something we could change to make my budget number possible?"

You may even offer ideas of a reduction in service or something along those lines, but let the owner respond to see what thoughts they have before going there. If they stand firm, thank them for their time and leave/hang up the phone. They may rethink their position, and this gives you time to think through your next step. Again, they may be the best and you call back in a couple days to sign on with them.

Commission Reduction Negotiation Strategy - Commission based payment structures call for a different approach. The commission structure likely exists because the company has interest in renting your vacation home. Many rental companies haven't embraced the rent by owner market and have high commission rates. Their standard commission structures are based on the marketing and guest service to book the reservations and all of the work to make things happen locally. The rent by owner model takes all of the marketing, booking, and much of the guest communication off their plates. So it stands to reason they earn less commission on those rentals. Fifty percent less is fair in this case, but give the rental company a shot at full commission for booking the rental if the rate is reasonable. Reasonable rental commission would be 25% or less. That way, they can treat it similarly to their other properties, and if they book it, they have a shot at earning more. If you follow the plan in this book, you are extremely likely to get it rented first and pay the lower commission. The rental company model could add to your success by putting a few more bookings on your calendar.

"I like the experience you create for guests, and it would go extremely well with rent by owner. I wanted to talk to you about a setup where we could both get bookings for the property, but you take care of all the local matters for all of my guests. Are you open to discussing a model like that?"

"Ok great, here is what I propose; I would pay your standard commission for the bookings you bring in of course. For bookings I bring in, I would pay half your commission rates for the local guest services. This would make sure you were compensated for the local services and adjust for the marketing and booking that I would do. How does this sound?"

If the owner insists on maintaining their rate structure, it isn't workable. A full commission for the local company will not maximize your rental income. So if this happens, keep looking. A counteroffer might be interesting, but anything much off your initial position ruins your economics.

You will want to find a deal you are comfortable with, and if one company doesn't work out just keep looking. It could be a long search, but don't be discouraged if your first few negotiations don't turn up what you had hoped. Making the experience great for your guests locally isn't easy, but is worth the time and effort to get it right.

The Contract

Once you find the right local partner, it's time to put everything in writing. Almost every company will put their standard contract in front of you and it's important to read every word so you know what you and the company are signing up for in the deal.

While you may be looking at a standard contract, it should often be tailored for your situation. There are three main areas to pay particular attention to during your review:

1. Services – A description of services is where the contract specifies what the local company will do as part of the deal. As you have unique guest experience requirements, this section will need updating. Make sure the services you require are described in the contract so everything is well understood. You may not need every service described, but make sure the list is as close to 100% as possible. This will avoid surprises down the road.

2. Indemnity & Insurance – Contracts may include provisions that indemnify the local company from financial burden in certain situations. In other words, indemnification means that if something bad happens the company isn't financially responsible. When properly and specifically defined, this indemnity may not be an issue. For example, if the local company had nothing to do with an issue on the property, they shouldn't be held responsible. The thing to watch out for is indemnity clauses that are too general. If the local company is looking to be protected against any issue on the property, this provision is too broad as they may be at fault. In general, the local company should be liable for issues they cause and not for issues they don't.

Also, keep an eye out for contract clauses that require specific insurance. As a practical matter, be well insured on the property including very strong liability coverage.

While not intended as part of the scope of this book, I highly recommend an umbrella policy in addition to the liability coverage that your rental home insurance provides. You never know what could happen that might create a lawsuit. Umbrella policies are not particularly expensive, and what peace of mind to know they could prevent your net worth from being completely wiped out by an issue on your property.

Lastly, make sure you understand the liability coverage of your local management company and what is covered. Your umbrella policy helps to cover your liability interests, but management company employees and damages should be covered by the management company's policy as appropriate.

3. Financials – The contract should clearly define how money will change hands in the agreement. Some straightforward statements in the agreement should do the trick. Using an example from a property management company, there may be a monthly charge and then additional charges that could apply for special services. The monthly charge should be specifically called out, and what is included in that charge is what is in the services section. If additional charges could apply, the conditions of these charges and amounts must be included. Contracts should protect both parties and provide a clear definition of the business relationship. The biggest thing to watch out for is general terms where additional charges may apply (such as repairs or oversight of repairs). This could quickly become a source of issue in billing where

unexpected charges could pop up that frankly could end the relationship. Maximizing rental income with increasing rental company costs is hard to do!

If the local company collects money from guests, make sure the contract spells out the schedule for payment to you. This should also include provisions to pay housekeepers if applicable and charges due to the local company. If the company holds your money for any period of time, you will be keenly interested in what day of the month they cut your "paycheck." Make sure this is spelled out and you hold them to it.

4. Termination – Very few folks go into a local partnership thinking much about the end, but even good relationships come to an end at some point. Flexibility and a smooth transition should the relationship end is critical to you and your guests.

Typically, either party can terminate the agreement. As long at the local company is making money from your business and they stay in business, chances are they won't terminate the relationship. Notice period is the amount of time prior to the last day of the relationship that the other party needs to be notified of desire to terminate. This should be a short period such as 30 days. Long notice periods should be avoided, as local performance may degrade if the company knows the relationship will end. Practically speaking, it takes a few weeks to get things undone anyway, like getting the cleaning company's linens out of the property.

The agreement should outline that a final date will be determined when notice to terminate is delivered. All company property is to be removed from the home on that date and any held money should be settled or distributed as well. It's also helpful to spell out in the agreement that services will be provided in the same manner and to the same degree of quality through the final day of the relationship.

This entire contract process shouldn't be particularly time consuming or difficult. Just read it a couple times and don't be shy with edits to get everyone on the same page right at the beginning.

Guests Finally Arrive!

Now is the moment your guests have been waiting for! Few moments are better than knowing you have your entire vacation in front of you. Since you made the arrival process super simple for them, they show up tired but are able to drive straight to your vacation home. Walking up to the front door, impressions begin to quickly form. Will it look like it did in the pictures? I sure hope it's clean! Folks may bring in a thing or two on their first steps into your home, but rest assured, they will take time to do a "tour." Who is sleeping in what room? It's time to look at the whole place and soak in these critical first moments that inform the impressions of the place. It had better be perfect.

Typically, you don't know the arrival time of each party, but most guests like to get every hour they can. An hour or so after your published arrival time, drop the guest a simple email. The email lets your guest know you want to make certain their vacation is off to a great start. It also welcomes communication if there is something the guest needs. Sometimes guests won't raise concerns and welcoming them makes sure that you can take care of anything they need. Lastly, the email reinforces that you have high expectations for their experience, and that you are taking time to make sure everything is just so.

You could have your local guest company reach out to them instead. I would not recommend doing both, as you will annoy your guest with too much communication. Oftentimes, local companies prefer to call guests; I try to avoid this unless I know the guest needs something. Phone calls are intrusive and especially so on vacation. A great percentage of the time the guest doesn't need a thing at that moment. If they did, chances are they would just reach out to you. Email is a great medium because guests can check it on their schedule.

The Goldmine Toolkit Arrival Email is extremely simple and designed to be a quick read. The first thing the email says is that you hope everything was just as it should be when they arrived. The second part of the message simply invites them to reach out should they need something. You aren't asking them to do a thing. Most guests respond, and because of the great local support they almost never need anything. The most common response I hear is, "Everything is great, thank you for checking on us."

From the point you send this email or hear back from the guests, leave your guests alone! They know how to find you and get that you want to help them have a great vacation. Occasionally, guests reach out; respond quickly. The guest issue could be anything from confusion on how to use the TV to a needed repair. I hope every owner reading this book has an iPhone or smartphone device. If you don't, please get one so you can monitor and respond to your email with lightning speed. Certainly, the phone feature is nice, but the email allows for the swiftest responses. The guest may choose email because they feel their issue or question isn't time sensitive. Wow them with a quick response and follow through.

Guests could be concerned about something that seems small but is big to them. One day, one of my guests shot me an email saying she thought the grass behind our place was a bit tall. At first glance, this seems a bit "nitpicky", but thinking it for a minute made it all make sense. This vacation property is on a golf course that can be easily accessed through the back yard. This is a major selling point of the property. I knew from prior email communications that the couple was avid golfers. Walking through somewhat tall grass in shorts is no fun. I immediately responded that the landscapers were usually quite good about keeping up with it and that I would inquire with the head of our Homeowners Association, which I did. I followed up in a couple hours to let them know I heard back and that the landscapers were headed over to take care of it. Clearly, this issue wasn't a huge deal, but there really was no reason for it and addressing it was easy. Give your guests the kind of follow through you would want!

Don't Wait For Complaints

All too often, I hear other owners or local company personnel talking, saying something like, "Well, no guests have complained about it yet." Another similar comment is "Let's keep an eye on that maintenance item, since we haven't heard from any renters about it." When it comes to Great local guest experience, never chance anything that could result in a guest complaint. Fix anything that could inconvenience guests in any way. Stay ahead of issues, from carpet cleanings to extermination, to make sure it's as close to perfect as possible.

When you receive a complaint, it's too late. Addressing complaints quickly and being responsive are good, but wasting time complaining about an issue and having to deal with getting it addressed robs your guests of valuable vacation time. Those few ants that found their way in might just get in that special dessert they brought and ruin the celebration. These certainly aren't the memories you want to create. Even if it costs you extra to fix it quickly, do it! Vacations with just fabulous memories are the ones that make for returning guests.

The Emotional Connection

Local guest experience done well clears the way for guests to connect or form a bond with your vacation home. Think for a moment about the emotional connection you have with your vacation home. You have a lot invested in it, both monetarily and in terms of effort, but there is more to it than that. You undoubtedly feel that the place is special. Also, I bet you have some great memories there. You can't force your guests to form an emotional connection to your home, but there are some things you can do to hopefully get them to feel similarly about the place. Ideally, your guests can feel like it's "their" place too.

During the marketing plan section, you made a list of special things about the property that make it unique. This is a great place to start. The view may be phenomenal and guests really want to get back to soak it in again while relaxing. The proximity to resort activities may be the best around. There are multitudes of possibilities. These special characteristics are important to highlight in a few different ways.

Guests can tell a lot about how you feel about the property through how you talk about it and your experiences there. Avoid overdoing it, but when answering a guest question, feel free to let them know about how much you and your family love an aspect of the property. Hopefully they, too, will feel this feature is special. You can also decorate the property in a manner that conveys special as well. You can get some paintings of your home and surrounding area done to enjoy and show your love of it. Thanks to fiverr.com, you can connect with artists who will do paintings for as little as $10-15. You just send them digital images of what you would like painted and typically, in a week, you will have a painting. Guests love local and regional décor that show a special kind of relationship with the vacation home. I have included a watercolor that I had painted of my lake property for $15 by an artist in Romania, which is located below.

Ancart, 12/3/2013

Another way to show your love for the property is to get a tasteful, personalized sign created. I recommend putting the property name/brand you use on your website and other guest materials. I also added a subtitle to mine that says "Welcome to Paradise." This clearly states that I feel my vacation home is paradise. This helps create a positive and special feeling about the surroundings. You could display this out front, but out back could be best to enjoy while hanging out. Etsy is a good place to find signs made to order. Just make sure it's properly sealed with outdoor polyurethane or something similar so it holds up to the elements.

The second, most important factor is great vacation memories. Thinking about the great times on vacation is fun and what you hope your guests will do. One step toward creating lasting vacation memories is a great local experience. The best way to help your guests create memories is to make activity suggestions. Make sure your suggestions include those that you remember most vividly. These suggestions are best delivered through the document you send to guests prior to their stay. Tell them the places you love and the things you love to do when there. Almost every guest appreciates suggestions for new things to do. For those that don't, that section of your document can be ignored. You will also get questions from guests for suggestions; use those opportunities to the fullest.

Nancy, one of my returning guests, has formed a very special emotional connection to our vacation home. She has been coming to our home every summer for almost 20 years. This is quite a bit longer than we have owned the property. She and her husband began vacationing there when their children were young. The children have since grown, and sadly, her husband has passed away. The adult children now bring their children and they and Nancy relive those vacation memories each summer. Our home has changed a great deal since we have owned it, but Nancy and her family have continued to come to "their" place through three owners. I wouldn't want it any other way.

The emotional connection can't be forced. It just happens, but you as an owner can do things to create a great environment for it to happen. The more you help it along, the more Nancy's you can get to fall in love with your vacation home.

Send a Thank You Postcard

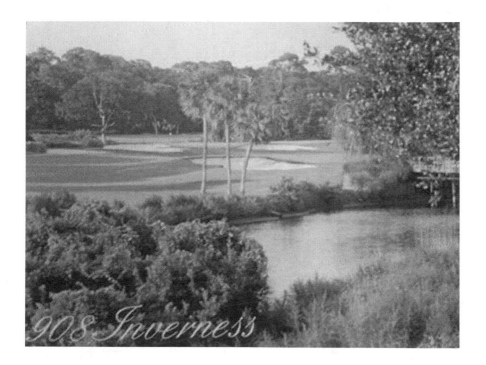

While your guest is vacationing at your home, send a thank you postcard to their home. Time it so that the card is waiting for them upon their return home or arrives a day or two later. The postcard front should be personalized to your property. Use the photo that shows the greatest asset or aspect of your vacation home. The idea is that the guest can relive and remember being there. Hopefully, they keep this to reference for next year. Who knows, it may end up on the refrigerator for a few months as a constant reminder of the awesome time they had.

Vistaprint has good pricing on photo postcards, which can make it quite inexpensive to get started. The design also allows you to put text on the front, so you can include your brand. Vistaprint also runs sales regularly. The note itself should be extremely short and handwritten. First, just thank the guest for coming to your vacation home. Then, tell them you hope they had a fantastic time and will come back soon. Sign it and you are done. Just takes a couple minutes and gives the guest something to remember their great vacation. The personal touch of a handwritten note from the owner speaks volumes about how much you care about them as guests.

After the Vacation – Harvest Testimonials & Reviews

Nobody wants a great vacation to end, but unfortunately, it must. Often, the guest has a long drive home and the best you can hope is that the excellent vacation memories make it just a little less painful. On the day of departure, send your guest a departure email. This email thanks them for staying at your vacation home and asks for their feedback. Clearly, you hope they just go on and on about how great everything was, but constructive feedback about what could be improved is often most useful. Phrase the request "Please let us know what was great and what could be improved." It's not complaining! Suggestions for improvement are a gift.

When you get suggestions for improvement, implement them if they make sense. You may get a lot of them. ALWAYS thank your guests for their feedback. If you implement one or more of their suggestions, let them know. This clearly demonstrates that you are listening to them and always trying to make your vacation home better. That's the kind of vacation home I want to go to! As an example, one of my guests said she had big trouble with the electric can opener, and would have appreciated a manual one. As soon as I read her suggestion, I jumped on Amazon and had one shipped Prime to my local company; it was in the drawer in two days. I sent her an email when it was in the drawer and thanked her for taking the time to let me know.

There's certainly no secret that great reviews are a big deal on listing sites, so get busy asking for some! Many of you may already do this, but I request a testimonial from each guest. I phrase it "If you had a great time, a few sentence testimonial would be great for prospective guests that are considering a stay."

201

No pressure. My hope is that the response to the email allows me to see the review before it's posted. Of course, do not attempt to instruct guests on what to say. Let the review in their words speak volumes about their experience. If the testimonial looks ready for a listing site, I ask that they post it as they wrote it to the listing site. I send over a link to make it easier. Almost everyone who takes the time to write a few sentences is willing to add it to the listing site.

Don't bother posting guest reviews yourself. Most discerning guests don't even read them, as they figure owners can sift through or change text. The only reviews worth having in my book are those in the words of your guests and provided by your guests. Do everything you can to make this process easy on your guests. The true gold in the goldmine is the guest reviews that talk about how you "thought of everything" and how "the owner was great to work with." These experience quotes are fantastic, as it's tougher to find that than a great view or roomy house.

Now that your guest is home and has provided their feedback and testimonial, this stay is complete. Congratulations, you just created a great guest experience for them. Onto the next guest!

The remainder of this book will focus on more owner-oriented topics, such as Using Data to Make Decisions and Vacation Rental Financials.

Gold Mining Tips

1. Invest in finding and paying for top-notch local service for your guests and you.
2. Make sure your local partner understands the differentiated guest experience you want to create.
3. Rental or concierge companies could fulfill this need; however, larger companies will generally be unwilling or unable to provide unique experiences.
4. Treat your local folks as partners and work together to continually improve the experience.
5. When searching for local support, ask questions about how they can bring your guest experience to life and conduct reference calls with the top contenders.
6. Make sure important terms are spelled out in the agreement and that the scope of services is clear.
7. Be proactive with property maintenance and do not wait for complaints to act. Often the damage is done when the guest has experienced the issue.
8. Tell your guests the property is special by how you talk about it and personalized décor.

Chapter 11 – Using Data to Maximize Rental Income

"Data! Data! Data! He cried impatiently.
I can't make bricks without clay!"

— Sherlock Holmes

How well is your system working? The famous saying goes, "I know half of my marketing spending is wasted, but unfortunately I don't know which half." Maximizing rental income isn't about spending lots of precious money on different listing sites. Instead, spend where the return is greatest. Without basic data, you are leaving money "on the table" and possibly overspending on lower return marketing. There are some very important questions to answer using data, which may show you the way to even more dollars from your vacation home.

1. How many bookings could I get a year?
2. Am I getting enough prospective guest shoppers to get the maximum bookings?
3. Am I doing a good job converting inquiries to bookings?
4. How many returning guests do I have year to year?
5. Where do my bookings come from?
6. Where should I consider upward or downward pricing adjustments?
7. Where do I stand financially from month to month?

The Goldmine Dashboard

The Goldmine Dashboard is the most powerful tool in the Goldmine Toolkit, and the purchase price is worth it for this document alone. The data you enter needs to be tracked so you can make sure everything is handled properly. The nerdy formulas are all built in, so you don't have to do the tough math to answer these questions yourself. The dashboard also displays the results graphically, making getting insight from the data that much easier.

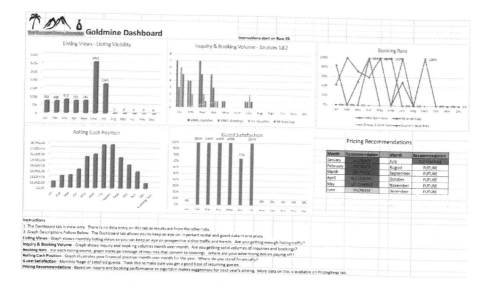

Each of the Tabs is designed to make it easy to enter and view the data in logical places.

Financials – This tab tracks how you are doing financially each month. Are you making money? Will you make money this year? You can check the table and graphs to see your performance for that particular month and rolling for the calendar year. If you aren't much of a finance person, the rolling financial pictures carries forward month after month so you can see how you are doing over the course of multiple months. There are line items for expenses like mortgage and HOA fees that you will need to enter each month. Some of the data is pulled automatically from other dashboard tabs. We will cover the financials tab in detail in the next chapter.

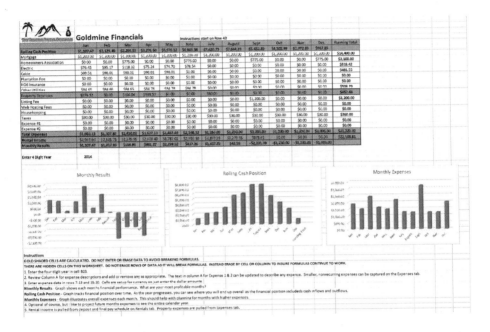

Inquiries – This tab keeps track of how you are doing with inquiries and bookings. You need to enter a few fields of inquiry data such as Name, Date, Travel Dates, and Inquiry Source. The charts are generated from this data and pulled from some other tabs. A rate calculator can be added to help with inquiry responses.

Rentals – This tab tracks rentals, payments, and all guest communications. You need to enter the fields including dates, email and physical address, payment information. This data feeds a lot of calculations in this and other tabs. As payment dates are coming up, the dates will be shaded yellow and then red as they are due. When you have lots of bookings, this coloration helps draw your attention to upcoming payments in case you need to take action. Guest communication dates are also shaded so you can stay on top of which communication should go out to guests. I look at the Rentals tab of the Goldmine Dashboard each morning to make sure communications are going out and payments are coming in on time. This keeps the vacation rental business rolling along!

Web Tracking – This tab tracks how many prospective guests are viewing your listing. Unfortunately, many of the top vacation rentals listing sites don't yet provide good dashboards on web traffic. That's a bit like being a shopkeeper who doesn't know how many customers come into your store. Many shopkeepers who don't track this kind of information, but those who do know a lot more about how to project their sales and make decisions about whether to advertise more.

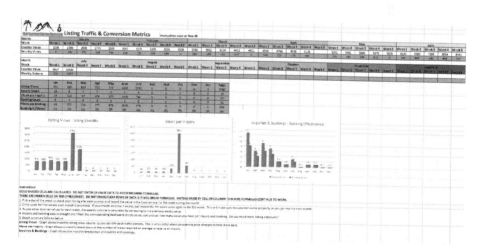

Here you can track the number of listing views, inquiries, and bookings. These views can suggest whether more listing exposure should be pursued to increase bookings. After tracking this data for a year, seasonal shopping trends can be seen. The time to edge your prices up for next year is before the highest shopping period. This gives you the greatest chances of landing bookings at higher rates. This also provides time for a pricing adjustment if the bookings aren't coming in at the new pricing.

Expenses – This very basic tab allows you to enter and track expenses. Anything from your listing expenses to home improvements to new coat hangers can be entered here. Line items entered here are tallied on the Financials tab automatically and figured into your monthly calculations. Staying on top of expenses is important discipline for your bottom line. If that isn't motivation enough, you need this information for your taxes each year. I print off the Expenses and Financials tabs from the Goldmine Dashboard for my accountant come tax time. This saves both of us countless hours trying to gather it at the end of the year. Who knows, if you have an accountant maybe he won't raise his rates because your taxes are so easy. Take the time to do this simple entry as you go. You will be glad you did!

Pricing Recommendations – The Pricing Recommendation tab suggests monthly rate adjustments based on booking performance. The algorithm examines booking volumes, inquiry to booking volume and reservation lead times. The algorithm identifies timeframes with the greatest opportunity to increase or decrease prices to maximize your rental income.

Rates – The Rates tab stores rates for each season for easy access so you can easily update your listing site, as timeframes age off the system.

Testimonials – The Testimonials tab is simply a spot to copy and paste all the great things your guests say about their experiences at your vacation home. Paste in the few sentence testimonials you get back from your guests, but also include the smaller compliments you get along the way. A good example would be an email response to the information you send over pre-arrival, such as, "Wow, you have thought of everything." These small tidbits can really add up! Once you get a few stacked up, you can add them to your website. I always send a note to the testimonial provider, letting them know I plan to post their comment and just want to check that it's ok with them. I suggest using first name and first letter of the last name to protect your guest's identity. Enjoy how fun and fulfilling it is to watch them stack up due to your great guest experience.

Using the Goldmine Dashboard Data – Lies, damn lies and statistics

While you are entering basic data in the Goldmine Dashboard, it is computing a lot of summary statistics that can be used to evaluate your vacation rental performance and make decisions to make you more money. If your data entry is solid, the numbers won't lie to you, however they can lead you to the wrong conclusion. Say, for example, you notice your Views per Booking number has gone through the roof lately. Does this mean guests have lost interest in my vacation home, or pricing is too high? As you sit and ponder how this could be when it was so great early in the year, it hits you. Your calendar is totally booked for the next six months, so it stands to reason guests are looking at your listing and moving on when they realize it isn't available for their timeframe. Just staring at one number could have you running off to list on more sites or tweak your listing.

The best way to guard against "over interpreting" the data is to use a lengthy timespan before declaring an issue or trend. Also, think of the data in the larger context of the number of bookable weeks. Often, changes in the data are explainable, so don't freak out if you see a month or two where numbers seem to have changed dramatically. Use the data like crazy to get at the extra dollars, but be careful!

Using Goldmine Dashboard data, examine each question from the beginning of the chapter to evaluate where the additional dollars may be.

Are your guests happy with their vacation experience?

The most reliable way to know this is to ask them, and many businesses use a survey to gather this information. For a vacation rental, a survey is more guest hassle than it's worth. You are already requesting a testimonial or review from each guest, which is what you really want to help boost your search position and bookings. Reviews can also be a way to measure guest satisfaction. When the review is requested, the guest is already home from their vacation. Traveling home and unpacking can be lots of work, and it would be easy for the guest to ignore your review request and just be glad the vacation work is done. Guests who take the time to write a few sentences for you are highly satisfied and likely to return. Hopefully, their testimonial says so!

For each guest who provides a testimonial/review, enter an "R" in the Review column of the Goldmine Dashboard – Rentals Tab. These entries will be counted to compute a Guest Satisfaction Percentage. Happy guests help your vacation rental marketing with their great reviews and help your bottom line with return visits.

Understandably, some guests just don't take the time to provide their feedback. They may be very happy, but unfortunately, you don't know unless they tell you. If the guest sends even a single sentence letting you know they enjoyed their vacation, go ahead and count it. Some folks just aren't very talkative. If you hear nothing, you are only left to believe they could be happier and don't count it.

The percentage of guests who let you know they are happy is your Guest Satisfaction Percentage. Since you are focused through this book to create a Great Guest Experience, set a high target for yourself and keep working towards it. A top-notch guest experience should yield an 80% or greater score. Push your goal up to 90% or higher over time as you continue to improve your guest experience.

How many bookings could you get a year?

Think of answering this question as setting a goal of how much time you could be rented. Ideally, you would rent every week, however that likely isn't realistic. Go through a year of seasons on the rental calendar and count how many bookings you think are possible. Be aggressive but realistic. If no one goes to your destination in the winter, don't count that time, but focus on being fully booked for all of the warm season weeks. Do some research on other popular properties on your listing site if you have questions about whether to include a particular season or month. After you tally it up, you have your bookings target.

If you are short of your bookings target, it is likely due to one or more of three causes:

1. Too few listing views – You may simply need greater exposure to guest shoppers to get more bookings. Look into increasing your subscription level or list on another high traffic site. If your Goldmine Dashboard Views per Booking number is high and you are well under your bookings target, bumping up your listing exposure may give you the lift you need.

2. Your listing needs work – An inquiry is a sign of guest interest, and if you are getting a reasonable number of inquiries, chances are your listing is generally effective. Conversely, lots of views and low numbers of inquiries is a sign that your listing isn't compelling. On the Goldmine Dashboard Web Tracking tab, a high Views per Inquiry number is a good indicator. Simply put, your listing isn't capturing your guest's interest. Many guest shoppers are viewing it, but no one much is biting. If you followed the listing guidance in earlier chapters, then it may be that your rates are out of line with the market. Study some competitive properties in your area to see where they are priced and booking. The Pricing Analyzer is a great place to start or revisit if previously completed. If your pricing is in line with the local market, take a hard look at your property pictures and other aspects of your listing.

3. You aren't effectively converting your inquiries – If you are getting a solid number of inquiries, but are well off your booking target, you aren't "closing the deal." This

situation yields a high View per Booking number and a low Booking percentage (Inquiry) on the Goldmine Dashboard. Your guest read the listing and was interested enough to inquire, but didn't book in the end. You may be in a highly competitive area, so look again at your pricing and whether you may have any policies that could prompt guests to shop elsewhere.

Are you getting enough prospective guest shoppers to maximize bookings?

The number of prospective guest shoppers varies greatly by vacation destination, and there isn't a magic number that works for all owners. Each vacation destination and property is unique. The Goldmine Dashboard Web Tracking tab shows the number of views it takes to get an inquiry and the number of views per booking. The Views per Booking measure is the most effective means to tell whether you need more exposure or views. Some math with that number can give you a general idea of whether you can hit your target with this exposure. Knowing your average number of listing views a month, figure out how many views you will likely get for the remainder of the year. Take this number and divide it by Views per Booking and that yields a number. See the math outlined below with an example:

How many views can you expect for the remainder of the year?
Average # of Listing Views Monthly x # of Remaining Months = Expected Views
800 Listing Views Monthly x 5 Remaining Months = 4000 Expected Views

Then, how many bookings could that mean?

Expected Views   /   Views per Booking   =   Projected Bookings

4000 Expected Views   /   800 Views per Booking   =   5 Projected Bookings

Please keep in mind that I used the word "could" to describe the number of projected bookings. Booking performance depends on several factors, and I suggest using this data to see whether things look in line or wildly off before deciding to spend more money on marketing. Investing brokers say it best: "past returns are not a guarantee of future performance." If your numbers look significantly off, it may be time to invest in some additional listing exposure.

Are you doing a good job converting inquiries to bookings?

A bunch of junky inquiries that don't turn into bookings waste your time. While each inquiry response doesn't take long, it adds up. Two graphs on the inquiry tab give you solid insight on this. First, look at the inquiry and booking volumes next to each on the Inquiry and Booking volume graph. On the sample below, you can see that VRBO outpaces HomeAway on both Inquiries and Bookings. A few months isn't long enough to call it a trend, however, keep an eye on HomeAway performance and make sure it's worth the money you are spending on it. If you do the US bundle, it doesn't take very many additional Bookings to make it worthwhile.

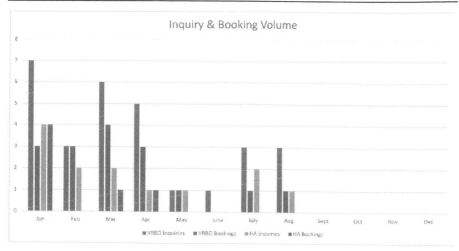

Another useful graph to look over is the booking rate. It simply graphs your percentage of inquiries booked over months. If your conversion rate is lagging, you may be losing out to lower priced properties. Give your pricing a hard look and make sure your listing and inquiry responses convey the value of your vacation home. Your listing site may just not be generating high quality leads. If you are on a major listing site, this is unlikely; however, some of the smaller sites have this characteristic.

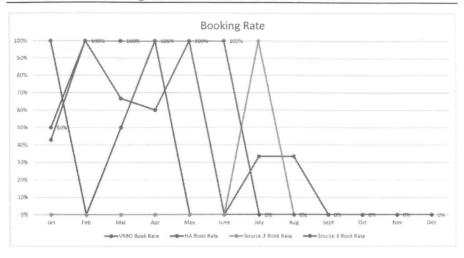

Where do my bookings come from and why?

Marketing expenditure needs to be considered in light of its return. High return sources are valuable and get rid of any low performers. Even if the listing site is cheap, it may not be worth keeping up with it if it isn't creating bookings. The Inquiry and Booking source tracking happens on the Inquiry Tracker tab. With every Inquiry you received, you recorded the source – HomeAway, VRBO, etc. The Inquiry and Booking volume graph on the right side of the tab is the most useful to see where the bookings are originating. If you have a listing source that is not producing over the long term, eliminate it. The booking rate graph can highlight high quality inquiry sources and those that may generate volume but not bookings.

The second part of the question is why your top listing sites are the best performers. That site could have the highest volume of vacationers for your area, or just the highest visitor volumes in general. On the other hand, perhaps you advertise at their top tier and the search placement drives big volume for you. You may not know for sure, but at least have a theory as to why what

216

you are doing is working.

How often are my bookings reservation requests?

This section is only for owners who decide to turn on a "Book It Now" option for guests. A high percentage of Reservation Request bookings is a good measure of listing quality. The guest was able to view your listing and website to learn everything they needed to know in order to book. No inquiry questions or email exchanges needed. This is easy for guests and easy for owners – just a few clicks and done! The Goldmine Dashboard Inquiries tab contains a column titled "Reservation Request." Tracking this is optional, but useful to watch. The Inquiry Tracker tab tracks a Reservation Request Rate.

Where should I increase or decrease my rates?

Pricing adjustments can be sensitive, but necessary to maximize your rental income. Rates set too low is money you could have in your pocket, and rates too high could mean fewer bookings. Both cost you money. Raise rates too high and you run the risk of fewer bookings. The logical question is "In what months/seasons should I change my rates and by how much? Since you are keeping a keen eye to the value your guests get for their dollars spent, I generally recommend modest increases through time, unless you have a significant pricing issue. Even small bumps in prices can really add to the bottom line throughout an entire season. So let's assume modest changes in rate, but where to make them? This is a topic where the Goldmine Dashboard data really helps.

On the Pricings Recs tab, you will find a graph and table that tallies rental results and uses what I fancily named the Rate

Adjustment Algorithm. In plain English, the Rate Algorithm looks for price increase opportunities by focusing on months where:

1. You got quite a few Bookings
2. The number of Inquiries received is similar to the number of Bookings
3. You booked well in advance of the vacation

In other words, the algorithm looks for timeframes where you booked easily and well in advance. This is a good situation to be sure, but it likely tells you that your price was so good that folks booked it up quickly; there is room to move it up.

Conversely, the algorithm also looks for price decrease opportunities. Not such great news, but if you can get more bookings with a small price decrease, it makes sense to do so. The algorithm for rate decreases is similar but simpler:

1. You didn't get a lot of Bookings
2. The number of Inquiries received was low
3. The number of Inquiries was greater than the number Bookings

The algorithm looks for months of low bookings and inquiries. If you didn't receive many Inquiries, it may very well be due to rates that are too high. In some cases, you may have received many inquiries, but guests ended up choosing other lower priced options.

On the Rates tab, the Rate Algorithm will colorize the month

Yellow if a rate increase should be considered. The month will be colorized red if a rate reduction should be considered. The algorithm doesn't handle monthly rentals gracefully, so you will need to ignore any months that you rent to the same guest for the entire time. Weekly and partial weeks work best.

Review each month and determine what changes you would like to make. You will need to decide what dollar amount adjustments you think make the most sense given the pricing analyzer and any other pricing research you may have done. It's ok to be the most expensive compared to similar properties, but you don't want to price out of the market. Go get that extra rental income!

How many returning guests do I have year to year?

Returning guests are a critical part of your vacation rental business. They tend to book early, which fills your calendar, and the returners take good care of your home. The Goldmine Dashboard Rentals Tab provides a Returner column for you to track how many returners you have month after month. For each reservation, just add an "R" to the Returner column and the dashboard will compute a Returner Percentage. This is simply the percentage of reservations for the month and year that are returning guests. You may not have many returning guests if you are just getting started. With a great guest experience, this should grow through time. Table and line graphs on the Pricing Recs tab help you keep track of progress getting that returner base.

Each year right after the Christmas Holiday, I recommend sending emails or postcards to each of your previous year's guests inviting them back. Postcards are best because they are tangible, with a great picture of the vacation home that reminds the guest of the fantastic time they had. This can be a significant volume of postcards, so a mail merge in Microsoft Publisher is an easy way to personalize yet print the postcard messages. When you send the communication, let the guests know you value them and that you want to offer them a rate that is lower than on your listing. Email is fine also, but can get lost in the sea of other emails the guest receives every day. In either case, all the info you need for a postcard or email "Come back message" is in the Rentals tab. Even if the guest doesn't book right away, they may let you know they plan to come back. This can open up a great dialogue where you can work together to find the timeframe that works best for them.

Tracking returners can help you better assess how well your guest experience is getting folks back to your home each year. A low percentage can prompt you to offer them better pricing, or do another mailing campaign to remind your past guests to come back.

Let the Goldmine Dashboard do the work to help you see how happy your guests are, and track your booking and financial performance.

Gold Mining Tips

1. Track and use data in the Goldmine Dashboard for decisions such as when to raise or lower your rates.

2. Determine whether you have enough prospective guest shoppers on your listing to book the available number of weeks. If not, make changes to get more views.

3. Look for trends in reservation requests and inquiry to bookings ratios to make sure you are converting bookings effectively.

4. Keenly watch the number of returning guests as building a base is critical to the Goldmine System.

Chapter 12 - The Financials of Vacation Rentals

"My goal wasn't to make a ton of money. It was to build good computers."
— Steve Wozniak

You may be wondering why a book about maximizing vacation rental income would cover financials last. Simple, financial performance is an outcome of everything else in the book. Your great guest experience creates loyal guests who come back, and through time, your prices rise for the new guests. It's supply and demand at its best that earns you more, while creating superb value for your guests. Great financials are not accidental or incidental, and require planning. Using the Goldmine Dashboard, you can track revenues and expenses without much effort. The biggest thing is to stay focused on entering the data. Well-managed tracking is worth its weight in gold. The data helps you make decisions on how to maximize your Vacation Rental Income. First, though, get clear on your financial goals.

Setting Your Financial Goals

Almost every owner strives to make big money on vacation rentals, and for some it's possible. Big profits on most vacation rentals year after year are rare. Depending on your current situation, set a more realistic goal, such as paying all of the mortgage or mortgage and expenses. There are many vacation homeowners who would love to get their vacation home annual expenses paid every year, enjoy their vacation home, and watch their asset appreciate. If you can make big money along the way, that's fantastic however I wouldn't realistically plan for that.

Think about what you are trying to achieve financially by renting your vacation home. Some owners just want to rent occasionally to help with basic expenses. While the goal is a personal decision, knowing it is critical. Your goal impacts every aspect of marketing and operating your vacation rental. If you want to pick up the occasional rental with limited wear and tear on your property, you are going to price, operate and market your rental very differently than if maximizing return is the goal. For most, covering the mortgage and expenses is a good goal to get started.

Financial Planning

Now that you have decided on your goal, put your financial planning into motion. Included with the Goldmine Toolkit is a document titled Financial Planning Worksheet. This spreadsheet gives you a simple way to model different rental scenarios against the expenses above to see where you will stand financially at year-end. If you have owned your property a while, you likely have a good idea of your annual expenses. The real trick is the rental income side of the equation, which will only be as good as your projections. As you make changes to your Guest Experience and Marketing, projecting rental income with precision is more difficult.

Use three rental income projections for planning purposes:
1. Conservative – Pick the lowest value as you can imagine for number of weeks and dollar amount for the year.
2. Likely – With additional marketing exposure, you will grow your rental revenues. Depending on where your starting point is, give yourself a solid percentage lift such

as 25%. To set a realistic percentage, make an estimate of how many available weeks are rentable. You can then take a percentage of that to get a likely number. Look at peak versus shoulder season rental revenues to figure out roughly how much you will charge for the additional rentals. This will help you get a more reliable dollar estimate. Picking up some peak season weeks will of course put more on your bottom line than off-season weeks.

3. Gangbusters – Looking at that same group of rentable weeks, your gangbusters scenario could be where you rent most of them. Translate those weeks into a dollar amount. If you weren't planning to go platinum level on your listing site, do adjust the expenses for that, as you will need to go big on marketing to make this happen. For Gangbusters projection, use the maximum number of rentable weeks.

So now what? These scenarios can help you with broader financial planning so you are prepared for feast and famine. Depending on your listing site plan, you may consider upping the ante to get the best shot at gangbusters. I highly recommend that approach. The scenario exercise can help you see big revenue upside for a small marketing investment with your listing site. If you haven't already, it's time to set your sights on going gangbusters!

Planning for Expenses

Vacation homes can bring significant expenses. Whether it's maintenance cost, Owners Association fees, taxes or insurance, it takes a lot to pay for your home away from home. Some of you may feel this all too well. These expenses also directly map to the financials spreadsheet in the event the description is helpful with tracking.

Some typical expenses to consider and estimate for your financial plan:

Property Taxes can quickly add up with reassessments. Some resort areas take the opportunity to dip into our pockets with non-resident rates. I find this interesting in that our rentals are the very thing that stimulates the local economy. It can really pay to understand how and how often properties are assessed for value in your area, so there aren't surprises.

Owners Association Fees can be a significant expense. While the dollar amount can be high, typically the value you receive by combining funds with your neighbors is high. Exterior maintenance including lawn care, landscaping, and painting are generally included. Just be glad you are renting to pay this bill.

Marketing Expenses include listing sites, website, and any other marketing expense. Done right, this will be at least $500-$1000 or more. Focus on the return you receive on this investment, and remember the saying: "You have to spend money to make money."

Maintenance is often a sizeable line item, but it depends on factors like how close you are to your property, whether you have a rental company, and how much maintenance you do yourself. I am not close to my properties, and I budget about $2500 a year in maintenance for each. This includes things like HVAC service, carpet cleaning, window washing, unforeseen fixes (towel rods coming off the walls, leaky icemakers, etc.). I am fairly handy so if it can wait, I will generally try to fix it myself. I don't wait on anything that would inconvenience a guest.

Utilities such as electric, cable, water, gas, etc., should be estimated for the year.

Special Fees or Assessments don't feel special, as they are typically unplanned expenses. Perhaps the most common is a Property Owners Association special assessment. If you have a POA, review the budget info and how often they have special assessments. Find out how much the POA keeps in reserve so you can assess the likelihood of a special assessment for upcoming expenditures. One of my POAs has very low dues but that brings special assessments each year that are tough to plan for effectively.

The second type is a utility special fee. For example, the public works in one of the areas I have a vacation property charges an extra quarterly fee for owners who rent. Their logic is that we overuse the sewer system due to our rental guests. I think they impose this fee because they can. Hopefully, you don't have these fees to worry about, but give it some thought to make sure your expense planning factors these in if appropriate.

Using the Planning Scenarios

Using the Financial Planning Worksheet, now you can see a range of annual rental income possibilities. The most important is the Conservative Scenario. Plan your personal financials to withstand this outcome. While not likely, being able to financially withstand the Conservative Scenario should help you rest easy at night. Spend some time looking at your Likely and Gangbusters scenario to see opportunities to boost your results. Should you boost your search placement by purchasing a higher listing tier? How about another listing site? A modest increase in marketing investment could yield a nice return. Also, study the expenses to see whether any trimming may be prudent. Just make sure not to cut anywhere that could compromise your Guest Experience.

How to Track Where You are Financially

The Goldmine Dashboard does much of the heavy lifting for you, but the dashboard depends on you to enter the expense data. Recurring expenses, such as your mortgage and homeowners association fees, can just be entered once on the Financials tab. Utilities will need a monthly entry and any miscellaneous expense should go on the Expenses tab. Data entered on the Expenses Tab is automatically pulled in for the appropriate month in a rolled up view on the Financials Tab. This is also true of the Rentals as the dollar amounts for Rental Income are tallied based on the payment dates on the Rentals tab.

The table and graphs on the Goldmine Dashboard Financials tab make it easy to know where you stand. As you move from month to month, you can assess how your property performs. The Financials tab also tallies a Rolling Cash Position to keep track of month over month performance through the year. Don't read too much into the Rolling Position in the early months of the year. By mid-year, the graph has a lot more meaning for the yearly financials. If you decide not to purchase the Goldmine Toolkit including the Dashboard, these values can be tracked through Microsoft Excel®. If you are skilled with Excel®

formulas, you can add up rental revenue and expenses for each month.

The discipline of budgeting and tracking actuals should eliminate financial surprises and make sure you don't overextend financially.

Taxes & Other Fun Stuff

Much has been made of the tax advantages of having a vacation home, but I have found the tax benefits to be fairly modest. To maximize rental income, owners should take full advantage of tax benefits that come with vacation rental ownership.

Start by keeping good records of all expenditures. This may sound obvious but the receipts can easily pile up (or disappear) and this task can be more difficult than expected. I keep a three ring binder for each of my properties to insure all utility statements and any other 8.5 x 11 documents are stored in chronological order. As the bills arrive, I log them in the Goldmine Dashboard for that month's tracking purposes. For small store receipts, I just keep a manila envelope and enter them on the Expenses tab. There are some nice apps out there for scanning and storing receipts as well if you prefer.

Here are some typical expenses that may be useful to consider to make sure you are getting the best tax advantage from your spend.

Marketing Expenses – Listing site costs, website hosting, postcards, postage
Operations Expenses – Cleanings, mileage for travel to your

vacation home for work trips, new housewares, utilities, HOA fees, repairs, cleaning supplies

Improvements – Any project materials, services provided, new furniture, appliances

Good recordkeeping throughout the year gets you ready for tax time without needing to pull an all-night session to get everything together.

Gold Mining Tips

1. Spend time on financial planning/tracking, as it is critical to maximizing your rental income.
2. Use planning scenarios for personal financial planning and decisions.
3. Decide your financial goals for renting your vacation home.
4. Plan for and track your expenses.
5. Use the expense tracking system that works best for you.
6. Track every expense to get the most at tax time and do it as you go.

Chapter 13 - Bringing It All Together

"Ideas are easy. It's the execution of ideas that really separates the sheep from the goats."

— Sue Grafton

This book is designed to give you the steps to get the greatest money from your vacation rental by providing great guest experiences. Work from the point of view of your guest, then go backwards to figure out the best experiences to provide.

Start with a simple, but great marketing plan for your property. Highlight characteristics that make your property unique to show guests why they should come to YOUR vacation home. Invest in creating a great listing (with awesome photos and reviews) and get the best search position possible in your destination area. Using the step-by-step plans, build a dedicated website that allows your prospective guests to really get to know your property and give you a professional looking "storefront." Keep up with maintenance of your vacation home and invest in improvements through time if needed to keep the technology and décor current.

Connect with your guests through thorough and efficient communications. Double and triple check the details to make sure you don't make mistakes and undermine guest confidence. Make the communications templates in the Goldmine Toolkit your own and communicate with purpose. Be flexible with guests where you can, and give proactive discounts to those you choose due to great demographics or tough to book timeframes. Always tell guests what is next and provide them rich information in advance of their arrival so they can plan. Make every experience as simple as possible for guests to minimize their effort.

Invest heavily in the local guest experience to find the right partner. Make sure you are on the same page on important topics like cleanliness and response, and do your homework on them to make certain they are capable of providing the differentiated experience you need. Do everything you can to make things easy on your local partner, so they can focus on your guests. Build a relationship with your local partner based on mutual gain so you can win financially together, and always communicate well.

Communicate with your guests via email so they know you are interested and that all is going well with their vacation. Take swift action to address any issues or questions. Appreciate your guest's stay with a request for feedback and handwritten postcard. Let them know how much you want them to return.

Stay diligent to enter the right information in the Goldmine Dashboard so you always stay on top of guest activities. The dashboard will also tell you where you stand financially and help you see opportunities to get more money from your vacation home. Review the dashboard daily to stay on top of communications and guest payments.

The great guest experience should create many returners. Take excellent care of these folks by keeping them one year behind the currently published rates. Edge the rates up in the peak season each year, and shoulder seasons as appropriate. Use the Goldmine Dashboard pricing recommendations to consider rate increases or decreases. As your place books with returners and lots of vacation shoppers, the laws of supply and demand support your pricing and put more money in your pocket. Listen carefully to the voice of your guests and never stop improving the guest experience. The Goldmine Toolkit gives you all the tools to make it happen. Get out there and get those dollars while your guests create memories they will never forget!

Appendix – Using the Goldmine Toolkit

The Goldmine Toolkit is designed to provide you, as an owner, all the tools to maximize your rental income. The kit includes everything from building your own property website to suggested pricing increases or decreases based on rental performance. This section gives an overview of each document and how to use it. While referenced throughout the book, the tools are available for purchase on www.vacationrentalgoldmine.com.

The Goldmine Toolkit is offered separately to keep the book price low. This affords readers low priced access to browse the system and ideas before purchasing the Toolkit. My hope is that you got many great ideas that you can implement for great guest experience at your vacation property. This system should net you thousands more in rental income. If you like the system and overview, please purchase the Toolkit and put it to work for you. I guarantee you will be satisfied, or I will refund your money in full.

Marketing & Financials

Goldmine Dashboard

The Goldmine Dashboard is the cornerstone of the Goldmine system. It tracks and monitors performance of all aspects of your vacation rental. This includes financial, inquiry, booking, and guest satisfaction performance. The Dashboard helps the owner stay on top of all guest communications and payments and recommends pricing adjustments. It requires the owner to enter basic inquiry, rental and expense data. It tallies performance results and graphs that help the owners make decisions that maximize rental income. The Dashboard is Microsoft Excel® based and includes the following tabs:

1. Financials – The Financials tab pulls information from Rental and Expense tabs to show a monthly and yearly financial view. It also allows the owner to enter utility and other expense items so that a full financial picture can be tracked. With this tab, you always know where you stand financially with your vacation rental.

2. Inquiry Tracker – The Inquiry Tracker allows owner entry of basic information on inquiries, such as guest info and timeframe. The outcome is also tracked to monitor booking performance. The Dashboard reports on information like inquiry volume, sources, and booking percentages. Booking performance can be monitored at a glance to measure listing quality and inquiry conversion to bookings.

3. Web Tracking – The Web Tracking tab provides visibility to insure your listing has enough prospective guests to get you bookings. Additionally, it shows weekly and monthly trends, which are extremely helpful when considering pricing adjustments (adjust prices before high traffic periods). Owner enters web counter information each week, and can see how many views per inquiry and booking to gauge listing and listing site effectiveness. This seems like a lot of work, however knowing when your guests are shopping is invaluable when you are considering price increases or decreases. If you miss a week or two, just estimate the week you missed, as you are looking for trends not precision.

4. Rentals – The Rentals tab tracks all critical information for guest reservations, and insures the owner is on top of all

communications and payments. Owner enters basic guest and reservation information. The dashboard colorizes important dates for payment and guest communications so the owner can focus on the important upcoming activities. Owner should look at this tab each day to stay current with key dates with this system.

5. Expenses – The Expenses tab tracks non-monthly expenses such as repairs or supplies. Enter just a few fields for each expense and monthly results are automatically tallied and included in the financials tab. Print this information out each year at tax time along with the financials tab and save the hassle of running around to gather documentation.

6. Pricing Recommendations – The Pricing Recommendation tab suggests monthly rate adjustments based on booking performance. The algorithm examines booking volumes, inquiry to booking volume and reservation lead times. Each month carries a red, yellow, or green pricing status. Green booking performance suggests no pricing changes. Yellow suggests that modest pricing increases should be considered for that month the following year. Red is a recommendation that pricing be reduced. Clearly, pricing adjustments can be considered for any month, but the algorithm is designed to point out timeframes with the greatest opportunity.

7. Testimonials – This simple tab gives you a single spot to store all the awesome guest feedback you receive. Use this for updates to the testimonials section of your website.

8. Rates – The Rates Tab is a convenient spot to store each season's rates and capture rate adjustments.

Vacation Rental Marketing Plan Template
The Marketing Plan focuses your marketing efforts on the aspects of your property that make it stand out from the competition. You identify the best aspects of your vacation home and those that could be better. The outcomes include points to emphasize in your pictures, listing text, website and guest communications. Additionally, you document where you plan to advertise and why.

Search Engine Marketing Worksheet
The Search Engine Marketing Worksheet assists with search engine research to determine the best places to advertise your vacation home. This focuses your marketing investment where the prospective guests are shopping!

Pricing Analyzer
The Pricing Analyzer helps set rental pricing by studying competitive properties in your area. The Analyzer incorporates owner assessments of Property Similarity, Booking Performance, and Guest Reviews. These factors identify heavily booked properties with great guest experience as a pricing benchmark. The Analyzer compares competitive pricing across the properties and compares yours to it. Outcome is pricing set with the benefit of the competitive property benchmarks. This may lead you to increase your pricing, and rental income.

Financial Planning Worksheet
The Financial Planning Worksheet allows you to plan your annual finances with three rental performance scenarios. It helps you identify and quantify expenses and project income across worst case, likely, and gangbusters scenarios. The output helps with personal financial planning and may lead to different marketing or

expense decisions.

Listing Planner

The Sample Listing Text provides an example of an experiential listing that can be modified for your property. The structure of the listing is outlined and can be easily reproduced for your listing.

Sample Rental Agreement

The Sample Rental Agreement is a simple two-page document that can be used in the VRBO reservation and approved electronically. Once your property information is updated, the agreement can be used verbatim, or modified to suit your needs.

Guest Experience & Communications

Local Guest Service Selection Worksheet

The Local Guest Service Selection Template helps you pick the best local service provider for your needs. After interviewing the owner or manager, score their question responses and may the best local company win! Questions can be added or deleted to meet your specific situation.

Guest Experience Worksheet

The Guest Experience Worksheet helps to simplify critical guest activities, like check-in, check-out, and getting help. Write the guest steps into each box for the current activity and then determine whether any can be improved or removed. Writing it down can really highlight opportunities.

Inquiry Response Email

The Inquiry Response Email provides the html email format, with spots for your property pictures and property brand. This will give you a differentiated inquiry response that you can customize for your property.

Email Header

The Email Header is a Microsoft PowerPoint® template for creating your custom email header. Modify the property name and include experiential property pictures.

Booking Email

The Booking Email is suggested content for guests when they book your vacation home.

Vacation Almost Here! Email

The Vacation Almost Here Email is suggested content for the email you send to guests a week before they arrive, with the Welcome to My Property Template.

Welcome To My Property Template

The Welcome to My Property Template tells the guest everything they need to know about your vacation home before they depart. Use the content for a hospitality app, should you choose to provide that service to your guests. The document suggests sections; however, it can be fully customized to your vacation home.

Arrival Email

The Arrival Email is suggested content to check in with guests just after they arrive to your vacation home to make sure everything is perfect.

Post Vacation Email

The Post Vacation email thanks the guest for vacationing at your home, asks for their feedback, and requests a testimonial.

Website

Create Property Website Instructions

The Create Website instructions give you everything you need to build a property website with no technical experience required. Step-by-Step instructions walk you through exactly what you need to do to build a great vacation property site. Link the site to your listing and let it help you close those bookings!

Homepage Design Worksheet

The Website Design Worksheet helps you design the homepage for your vacation property site. Complete this worksheet before creating the website to make certain you know what content to include and why. Decisions include what pages, pictures, and text to include.

All Other Webpages Design Worksheet

The All Other Webpages Design Worksheet helps you design the remainder of the pages. Complete a worksheet for each page and you are ready to create the site.

The tools will be updated from time to time as needed, so feel free to check back to the site with your login to see if there are new versions. Each document name includes a version number for easy reference. Instructions are included at the top of each document. Read each instruction before starting with the tool. Stumped or have a question? Just email chris@vacationrentalgoldmine.com and I will do anything I can to help. I hope you can use these practical tools to bring many more dollars to your bottom line!

Made in the USA
Lexington, KY
07 November 2018